TRUE
SURVIVAL
STORIES

TRUE
SURVIVAL
STORIES

ANTHONY MASTERS

STERLING PUBLISHING CO., INC.
New York

Library of Congress
Cataloging-in-Publication Data Available

10 9 8 7 6 5 4 3 2 1

Published in 1997 by Sterling Publishing Company, Inc
386 Park Avenue South, New York, N.Y. 10016

Originally published in Great Britain in 1997
by Robinson Publishing Ltd

Distributed in Canada by Sterling Publishing
c/o Canadian Manda Group, One Atlantic Avenue, Suite 105
Toronto, Ontario, Canada M6K 3E7

Printed and bound in Great Britain

Sterling ISBN 0-8069-9657-9

CONTENTS

CONTENTS

CONTENTS

To my dear friend Tom Clarke
who fought the most heroic survival
battle of them all

CHAPTER 1

117 DAYS ADRIFT

Maurice and Maralyn Bailey spent a total of 117 days adrift in the Pacific when their yacht was struck by a whale on 4 March 1973, near the Galapagos Islands. The badly damaged boat sank and all they had left was their small life raft and rubber dinghy. After the rations the couple managed to salvage were used up, the Baileys became completely dependent on food from the sea and water from the sky.

Fortunately the area round the shipwreck was rich in fish and turtles, but Maurice and Maralyn had to find ways of fishing and trapping that tested their inventiveness to the full. The Baileys' ordeal is, so far, the longest of any human beings cast adrift. They were forced to survive in horrendous conditions, and the fact that they managed to do so was due to their resourcefulness and compatibility.

As the *Auralyn* went down and the whale, already wounded, had swum away in a trail of blood, the Baileys tried to collect what they could from the objects bobbing up and down on the water. They had already spent just under an hour taking what they could from the cabin. Later, doing an inventory, they listed the following survival items for the coming days:

SALVAGED EQUIPMENT

* = items left when rescued

2 blue bowls*
1 round bucket
1 oblong bucket*
1 plastic wastepaper
  basket
2 cushions
2 towels
1 camera*
2 sail bags*
2 oilskin jackets and
  trousers*
1 binoculars
1 tilley lamp
1 mallet
1 sextant*
1 compass
2 books
2 dictionaries*

1 Camping Gaz stove*
1 torch
1 scissors*
1 pliers*
2 plates (1*)
2 mugs (1*)
2 saucepans (small) (1*)
1 bag clothes*
1 neck-watch*
navigation books*
ship's papers and Log*
2 diaries*
mariner's knife and
  marlinespike
1 box safety matches
2 pencils
1 felt pen (found in
  Maralyn's oilskin
  pocket)

Emergency bag including: First-aid kit, knife, fork
and spoon each, penknife, small walking compass,
vitamin tablets, glucose, Heinz baby food, nuts,
dates, peanuts, water bottles (and should have
contained fishing equipment).

SALVAGED FOOD

2 tins steak and
kidney pie filling
1 tin Ambrosia rice
pudding
2 tins Fray Bentos
steak and kidney
pudding
2 tins Tyne Brand
minced beef
2 tins Wall's braised
steak
1 tin Sainsbury's
ravioli
1 tin curry
3 tins sardines
1 tin Wall's pork
luncheon meat
1 tin ham and egg roll
6 tins Campbell's
spaghetti bolognaise
1 tin Blue Band
margarine

2 tins Carnation
evaporated milk
2 tins Carnation
condensed milk
1 tin Tate & Lyle treacle
1 tin Big-D peanuts
4 tins Heinz baby foods
1 packet Whitworth's
brazil nuts
Half packet dates
1 bottle Boots multivite
vitamin tablets
Half jar Carnation
Coffee-mate
Half jar Robertson's
marmalade
4 packets Carr's
biscuits
Half small jar Boots
glucose powder
1 Huntley & Palmer
Dundee cake

This makes a fascinating list for the imagination, but in reality their provisions were desperately inadequate for 117 days. However, as they were comparatively near the shipping lanes, neither Maurice nor Maralyn anticipated drifting undetected for so long.

Initially, the Baileys found *Auralyn's* shipwreck emotionally shocking. They had both left mundane jobs to make the voyage and had lived on the yacht while renovating and repairing her.

She symbolized freedom, and had carried them safely for many thousands of miles. She was their home.

Nearly four months of drifting, of sighting ships but not being seen themselves, of suffering enormous weight loss and in Maurice's case severe illness, debilitating sores and a constant struggle against loss of morale, should have killed both of them. But it didn't. In the end their resolution and resourcefulness prevailed.

Another reason for the Baileys' survival could well be the fact that mentally they deliberately only lived one day at a time. After so many days of successfully sailing *Auralyn*, the Baileys were already part of the ocean environment. They coped as if they were true creatures of the sea, rather than land-locked human beings. Maurice writes of the sinking of the yacht:

It was heartbreaking. Auralyn *had been more than just a boat to us, she had been a friend and companion – our home. There was no recrimination, Maralyn was wonderful. She did not blame me for our desperate plight. Yet I blamed myself and I probed my mind to find exactly what I had done wrong. Was there something more that I could have done to have saved the ship? Everything appeared confused just before we abandoned* Auralyn *and now with that clarity generated from hindsight I imagined that, with a little more effort, I could have saved her. I think that I was mistaken, nothing could have saved that boat.*

Maurice wondered if the whale had been harpooned by a whaling ship they had sailed past just before the shipwreck. Had the whale, already wounded, somehow escaped the harpoon and taken revenge on the *Auralyn*?

Later, alternative theories suggested the whale could have mistaken the boat for another of its kind, or that the great creature had taken against the red anti-fouling on the hull, but the Baileys stuck firmly to the original explanation.

Maralyn recorded:

Our world was now so small. I arranged the few possessions we had salvaged round the outside of the raft so as to leave room in the centre for us to sit. After the initial burst of tears, I was only able to think of the matter in hand and found it easier if I concentrated on the present task.

We stayed around the immediate area for quite a time and picked up a few items which had floated up from the depths, but surprisingly, very little wreckage appeared. Maurice rowed the dinghy back and forth and picked up two pencils, a tin of margarine, a jar of Coffee-mate, a small container of methylated spirits, one gallon of kerosene and four water carriers each containing one gallon. We were pleased to pick up the water as it increased our meagre supply. Maurice had only managed to get six gallons into the dinghy before the boat had sunk but now we had ten.

The only two books that Maralyn had managed to salvage from the yacht were Eric Hiscock's *Voyaging* and a biography of Richard III by Paul Kendall Murray. They were both to know these two books in intimate detail, reading and then discussing them, squeezing out every possible drop of interest.

Maurice, who had salvaged all his navigational aids, plotted that their position was 1 deg 30' N, 85 deg 47' W, 250 miles north of Ecuador and 300 miles east of the Galapagos Islands. Unfortunately, this was too far north to allow the western current to drift their little flotilla over to the islands.

The wind was blowing from the south-east, and although it wasn't strong he knew it would drive them even farther north. Maurice wondered if they could row the hundred or so miles south to the latitude of the Galapagos. It would take approximately twelve days to reach their longitude, drifting at an average speed of twenty-five miles per day. This meant they would have to row ten miles per day south so as to offset the wind and current and to reach their latitude at the same time as attaining the longitude. Naturally, his calculations depended to a large extent on the wind and current remaining constant. Were they capable of rowing the dinghy ten miles each day with the raft in tow, or should they abandon the raft to give themselves a better chance?

Maurice did not pass the bad news on to Maralyn immediately because he was sure they would drift into the shipping lanes and be picked up. After all, they had flares, didn't they? But he had overlooked how small they were in relation to the swell, and even with the flares they would be hard to spot unless the ships came very close by – which they didn't.

Worse still, they both noticed that the raft had lost some air pressure, and as Maurice pumped up the tubes he realized how utterly vulnerable they were.

Supplies of water they had rescued from the yacht were obviously limited, and the scorching heat made their ration of one pint a day intolerable. More disaster soon struck when Maurice discovered that the water in the containers in the dinghy had been contaminated by the sea. The shock of the shipwreck was over and so was the numbness. The Baileys were quickly realizing the full horror of their position.

They began to row the dinghy at night, trailing the inflatable behind, but it was an arduous and unrewarding task, slow and sluggish because of the towing. They rowed for eight hours, their thirst unslaked, despite taking the risk of doubling their water intake.

For three nights they rowed in turn, each taking a two-hour shift. The Baileys had taken the *Auralyn*'s compass from her cockpit and Maurice had wedged it between the water carriers. As a result, they were able to follow a course, although this was dependent on moonlight. When they had no moon, the steering could only be done by the stars.

At the end of the night the Baileys were both exhausted, with blisters on their hands and a monumental thirst. They were already drinking far too much for their meagre supplies to last for long and Maurice soon had to reduce the ration to one pint of water each per day. He reckoned this was about the least amount their bodies would need without dehydrating.

At this point Maurice knew he had to dash his wife's hopes. He was forced to explain the true position, pointing out that they had only managed to gain ten miles south by rowing, and would have to continue for at least another ten to twelve days to reach the latitude of the Galapagos Islands. Unfortunately, however, the current was taking them west faster than they rowed south, so however hard they rowed they would still pass north of the Galapagos Islands.

The Baileys' ordeal was made ever more painful by the sighting of ships, the lighting of flares and the grim sight of the ships sailing away. Nothing could be more frustrating, and as time went on they both began to believe they were dogged by ill-fortune, made deliberately invisible, enduring their torture in complete isolation.

To make matters worse, the gas cylinder had run out and the remainder of their salvaged tinned food would have to be eaten cold. Psychologically this was bad; even more frightening was the knowledge that the food itself would eventually run out. Desperation, however, made the Baileys resourceful, and they decided that they would vary their diet by killing one of the turtles which continually bumped against their raft. Initially they had been against this, anxious not to prey off any of the creatures of the ocean, but their survival instincts took over.

Eventually they managed to capture a turtle and pull it over the side of the dinghy. Their instruments were simple but lethal – a blunt stainless steel mariner's knife, a pair of scissors and a steel penknife that had been sharpened up by being honed on a leather sheath.

The reptile lay on the floor of the dinghy without struggling, but Maurice knew he would have to knock it into unconsciousness before making his attack. The only way to kill the creature was to cut its throat, or decapitate it, and Maralyn also realized that she would have to undertake the operation while Maurice held the turtle still. She didn't want to be the executioner, particularly as the creature seemed so friendly and helpless, but she knew they had to live.

Eventually, Maurice stunned the turtle by hitting it over the head with a paddle, holding it upside down on the dinghy thwart, its head hanging down over a bowl. Maralyn then began the gruesome task of slitting its throat. The first stroke of the knife made no impression at all and she took a long time to hack even a small gash in its rubbery throat.

As they struggled, the turtle came to life again

and began to flail around with its flippers and claws. Unreasonably, Maralyn felt angry with the creature for making the job even more difficult, and Maurice had a hard task to hold the turtle in place. It took a tremendous effort to keep the neck stretched out. When the head was partly severed Maralyn dug for the arteries and rich blood spurted over her hands as the turtle gave up.

The bowl quickly filled with thick red blood, and although the Baileys had read of people drinking turtle blood, the idea was so revolting they emptied the bowl into the sea. At once, hordes of fish converged on the dinghy and began eating the congealed blood, making loud sucking noises as they devoured the contents of the bowl. Maralyn had difficulty washing her hands as the fish swam towards her fingers.

The next part of the surgical operation was to remove the lower shell. After deeply scoring the perimeter, Maurice cut through with the penknife. They then prised both halves of the shell away, exposing the rich white meat. Maralyn managed to hack four large steaks from each shoulder blade and they pushed the remains of the carcass overboard, delighted that the carnage was over.

They used the turtle meat that couldn't be eaten as bait. Unfortunately, there was no fishing equipment in the emergency bag, so they made a fishing line of cord and hooks by cutting stainless steel safety pins and bending them into shape. The catch was plentiful, and although it had to be eaten raw, the Baileys were so hungry that they hardly noticed.

Fishing was an evening ritual, and to keep themselves occupied during the day they read their two books, taking turns at reading a page out loud. They would then have a discussion, a game of cat's cradle, word games and home-made dominoes and cards.

The Baileys also rigged up a device to catch the always elusive rain water, managing to get the precious liquid to run down a canopy into a vent chute. It was then collected in a bucket and baled out with a mug into a series of bottles and containers. This was yet another example of how to avoid panic and think ahead, using wits to devise some ingenious ways of staying alive.

As day succeeded weary day, however, despite the diet of turtle meat and fish, the Baileys were rapidly losing weight and Maralyn noticed her husband becoming dramatically thinner. His ribs showed and his cheeks were sunken, his whole face having a gaunt appearance that was enhanced by his rapidly growing beard. They were also losing their tan, for it was essential to keep out of the sun as much as possible.

When Maralyn and Maurice had left Panama

they had no excess fat on them at all, weighing 118 pounds and 158 pounds respectively. They seemed to have lost weight very fast during the first month and then the rate of loss slowed down. They didn't have a mirror, but after much persistent questioning, Maurice told his wife that her face also looked very gaunt. The bruise she had received on her cheekbone had gone, but her shins were badly bruised, tender from the knocks she had received when leaving the sinking yacht. Worse still, their limbs appeared wasted and Maralyn wondered just how long their leg muscles would be able to support them.

Water was still a major problem, as they had had little rain in the first month and the heat was intense. Their lips became dry and cracked and the small sips they allowed themselves from the water flask didn't help much. In fact it made them feel worse. They ate fish, which helped to alleviate their thirst a little, but the diet was monotonous and they longed for more turtle meat. They began to dream of the succulent steaks, obsessed by the feast they might have. Gradually, however, their skills grew and they began to catch more of the creatures.

Towards the end of the first month, the Baileys had a sudden idea. They caught a large male turtle and held him upside down in the water, placing two half-hitches around his feet. To their great surprise, when gently placed upright again the turtle towed the flotilla in the direction of the Galapagos Islands. In fact he towed them so strongly that a considerable bow wave was created.

The turtle's unexpected help seemed like a miracle, but when the Baileys assumed that two or even three harnessed turtles could tow them faster, they discovered this was not to be the case, largely because the next turtle they tried perversely towed them in the opposite direction to his companion.

Missing ships, rough weather, despair and exhaustion overtook the Baileys in the second month. They contemplated suicide but Maralyn, the more optimistic of the two, always believed they would eventually be rescued.

Despite her hopes, they had noticed a split had occurred in the tape joining the two circular tubes at the front of the life-raft, which was hardly surprising considering the battering it had received, particularly from the turtles. There was nothing they could do to make a repair and it became essential to move with extreme care inside so that the split wouldn't widen.

Bad health was to follow, and after both the Baileys had suffered a mild attack of dysentery, Maurice had a much worse illness with pains in his chest and a persistent cough. He was cold, feverish and light-headed, symptoms that reminded him all too clearly of a bout of pleurisy

he had had some years ago. Somehow he survived and nourishment was heightened by the
capture of a female turtle whose eggs they ate.

The Baileys became even more obsessed with
food, turtle meat being the 'treat' they most
desired. Now they began to search for female turtles, recognised by their short tails, because they
had discovered their livers were sweeter and
bulkier than those of the males. They would also
discuss more civilized meals that they might eat
at home or in France, and Maralyn wrote down
recipes in her diary.

Gradually they had the mystical feeling that
they belonged to the sea itself and they would
never again reach dry land. Sharks rammed the
flotilla, storms battered them and salt water
sores on their bodies made daily living painful
and utterly miserable.

Then, on their 118th day (30 June), they once
again sighted a ship. Despite their desperate
waving, at first it looked as if, like all the others,
she was going to sail past. Then, to the Baileys'
numbed disbelief, she came back; a Korean fishing vessel that eventually manoeuvred herself
into the wind to come alongside, not only to pick
up the Baileys but also their two noble craft.

Once on the deck of the ship they were too
weak to stand and couldn't sit because of their
sores. Although the captain, Suh Jung Il, was

afraid the Baileys were Russian, he looked after them with great compassion, feeding them European food and ensuring they were cared for medically. The ship, *Weolmi 306*, engaged in tuna fishing, eventually returned them to Korea.

Whilst on their voyage they would rest in their cabin, hardly able to believe their luck, greeting members of the crew as they passed by. Many would stop to deliver gifts, such as toothpaste, clothes, soap, toothbrushes, chocolate, biscuits and cosmetics. The Baileys were deeply touched by their generosity, guessing that some of these presents had been intended for their families in Korea. Later, the bosun made them a gift of the only two belts he possessed to help keep up their trousers.

Even more generously, the captain and crew volunteered to deny themselves the luxuries of chicken, beef, water-melon, pineapple, milk, eggs and bread so that there would be enough 'European' food for the Baileys.

The ordeal was over, but could never be forgotten or even locked away in the back of their memories. Maurice and Maralyn Bailey had become part of the sea, hunting and fishing like members of a primitive tribe. Had they not had the courage and adaptability to live in this way, the Korean fishing boat would have found only an empty dinghy. The Baileys would have become part of the ocean's food chain themselves.

CHAPTER 2

ERNEST SHACKLETON IN THE ANTARCTIC

Shackleton was the greatest of all British polar explorers, making no less than three expeditions to the Antarctic. All of them were traumatic. He was invalided back from the first (1901–4), which was led by Scott who was to eventually die there. In his second expedition (1907–9) he was forced to give up when he was just under a hundred miles from the pole. At the beginning of the third (1914–16), his ship, the *Endurance*, was crushed in the ice before he could begin the long and dangerous trek across the snow.

Shackleton was the son of a South London doctor. As a young man he joined the Royal Navy but he was by no means a pillar of the establishment. Always an individualist, he was a rebel who hated the then snobbish paternalism of the Royal Geographical Society, and while on his expeditions went out of his way to break down the social barriers between its members. Nevertheless, there was no doubt that Shackleton was highly patriotic and wanted to do his best for his country. The major quality he insisted on was loyalty and if betrayed he was unlikely to forgive the betrayer.

The second attempt to reach the South Pole was hazardous in the extreme, yet Shackleton's enduring leadership inspired the expedition under the most appalling conditions. He always drove himself hard, although his physical fitness was flawed by a heart murmur which was to lead to an early death from a coronary in 1922.

Shackleton's intention was that this second expedition should leave New Zealand at the beginning of 1908 and sail to winter quarters in the Antarctic. To avoid being frozen in, some members of the expedition, together with the stores, would be landed and then the ship would return. The shore party was to winter with sufficient equipment so that three separate groups would be able to start in the spring.

The first would go east towards new territory, known as King Edward VII Land, and follow the coastline. They would return when 'it was considered necessary to do so'. The second group would proceed south, keeping fifteen to twenty miles from the coast, so that rough ice could be avoided. The would might go westward over the mountains, and instead of crossing in a line that was due west would head towards the magnetic pole.

The programme was both complex and ambitious, but Shackleton was confident as he had selected his expedition members carefully. The ship, *Nimrod*, set sail, and by 3 February was ready to land the stores. She departed again at five o'clock on the afternoon of 18 February in a howling blizzard.

Shackleton gives a vivid account of the conditions in the heart of the Antarctic:

'All night the gale raged with great fury. The speed of the gusts at times must have approached a force of a hundred miles an hour. The tops of the seas were cut off by the wind and flung over the decks, mast and rigging of the ship, congealing at once into hard ice, and the sides of the vessel were thick with frozen sea water. "The masts were grey with the frozen spray, and the bows were a coat of mail." Very soon the cases and sledges lying on deck were hard and fast in a sheet of solid ice, and the temperature had dropped below zero. Harbord, who was the officer on watch, on whistling to call the crew aft, found that the metal whistle stuck to his lips, a painful intimation of the low temperature.'

Later, the weather cleared and the wind dropped as *Nimrod* moved slowly away from her icy berth, leaving the shore party in the recently constructed hut to await her return in the spring.

Shackleton was himself to make the southern journey, along with three other men – Adams, Marshall and Wild. The specially adapted motorcar was discovered on testing not to be able to travel over soft snow so they took the ponies, with provisions for ninety days.

SHACKLETON IN THE ANTARCTIC

It is interesting to note the daily allowance of food each man was allowed to have:

	OUNCES
pemmican	7.5
emergency ration	1.5
biscuit	16.0
cheese or chocolate	2.0
cocoa	.7
plasmon	1.0
sugar	4.3
Quaker Oats	1.0
	34.0

The personal clothing worn by each member of the expedition was as follows:

> woollen pyjama trousers
> woollen singlet
> woollen shirt
> woollen guernsey
> two pairs thick socks
> one pair Reindeer skin boots (finnesko)
> burberry overalls
> balaclava
> burberry head covering
> woollen mittens
> fur mittens

The men also had a bag which weighed seventeen pounds and, in addition to letters, diaries and personal possessions, contained:

> pyjama sleeping-jacket
> pyjama trousers, spare
> eight pairs woollen socks
> three pairs finnesko [boots]
> supply sennegrass
> three pairs mittens
> spare woollen helmet
> one pair ski-boots
> woollen muffler
> two pair goggles, one smoked,
>   one coloured
> roll lamp-wick, for tying on mitts
>   and finnesko
> sledge flag
> tobacco and matches

The difficulties of travelling over snow in poor light were immense. When there is cloud or mist no shadows are cast on the dead white surface which then appears to be uniformly flat. Snow mounds and small depressions are therefore invisible and highly dangerous to both men and ponies. Also, the strain on the eyes under such conditions is enormous, and the likelihood of snow blindness increased.

This complaint is particularly painful. It begins with a runny nose and continues with double and later blurred vision. The blood vessels of the eyes swell, the eyes water and begin to close completely. The only way to guard against an attack is never to remove your goggles. At the time of Shackleton's expedition the only cure was to drop cocaine into the eyes and then to apply a powerful astringent, like sulphate of zinc, to reduce the swelling of the blood vessels.

By 20 November, the expedition met a surface that was the worst they had encountered so far. It was terribly soft, but they managed the statutory 15 miles 800 yards per day.

They were exhausted that night, but the ponies were all fit except for one called Chinaman, and he would have to be shot the next day. He was now unable to keep up with the others, and the bad surface had finished him off.

On Christmas Day the four-man expedition had a feast, temporarily masking the fact that the going had been much slower than they had planned. It consisted of pony ration boiled up with pemmican and some of their emergency Oxo and biscuit. In the cocoa water Shackleton boiled a small plum pudding, which a friend had given them. This, with a drop of medical brandy, was a great luxury. Then came the cocoa, and finally cigars and a spoonful each of crème de menthe sent from Scotland. The expedition had full stomachs that night but they all knew that this would be their last big meal until the end of the trek.

After dinner, grim reality took over and they discussed the present position. They had five hundred miles to go — the distance between the area they were now in and the pole they had to reach and then back again. They had one month's food, but only three weeks' biscuit so the decision was made to reduce rations and make each week's food last ten days. They could also have one biscuit in the morning, three at midday and two at night.

By 30 December, however, the expedition was in considerable trouble. Blizzards were slowing them down badly, leaving very soft snow on the

surface. Soon the drifting was so bad that they had to camp, lying in their sleeping bags and trying to keep warm. The following day they were back in action but Shackleton wrote in his diary:

December 31. The last day of the old year, and the hardest day we have had almost, pushing through soft snow uphill with a strong head wind and drift all day. My head has been very bad all day, and we are all feeling the short food, but still we are getting south. We are in latitude 86 deg 54' South tonight, but we have only three weeks' food and two weeks' biscuit to do nearly 500 geographical miles. We can only do our best. Too tired to write more tonight. We all get iced-up about our faces, and are on the verge of frostbite all the time. Please God the weather will be fine during the next fourteen days. Then all will be well. The distance today was eleven miles.

Gradually Shackleton was beginning to accept that they were running out of time, and after all their efforts the prize of planting the British flag at the South Pole might in the end elude them. By 4 January, he realized that because the members of the expedition were weakening so quickly, they could only continue for three more days at most. The southern blizzard wind, the shortage of food and 46 deg frost were making enormous inroads into the expedition's spirit. The altitude was now 11,200 feet, and because of the savage wind, their faces were cut and their feet and hands always on the verge of frostbite.

On 6 January, Shackleton's diary entry makes it clear that the expedition had finally accepted failure:

January 6. This must be our last outward march with the sledge and camp equipment. Tomorrow we must leave camp with some food, and push as far south as possible, and then plant the flag. Today's story is 57 deg of frost, with a strong blizzard and high drift; yet we marched 13 and a quarter geographical miles through soft snow, being helped by extra food. This does not mean full rations, but a bigger ration than we have been having lately. The pony maize is all finished. The most trying day we have yet spent, our fingers and faces being frostbitten continually. Tomorrow we will rush south with the flag. We are at 88 deg 7' South tonight. It is our last outward march. Blowing hard tonight. I would fail to explain my feelings if I tried to write them down, now that the end has come. There is only one thing that lightens the disappointment, and that is the feeling that we have done all we could. It is the forces of nature that prevented us from going right through. I cannot write more.

Next day, a blizzard shrieked around them, blotting out the landscape, and the temperatures ranged from 60 to 70 degrees of frost. The men were forced to lie in their sleeping bags all day as fine snow was blasted through the sides of the worn tent.

If the wind dropped, Shackleton's plan was still to march south as far as they could get, plant the flag and then turn back towards home. Their chief anxiety was that their tracks might have been obliterated by driving snow. Without them they would not be able to find their way back to base, for there were no land bearings that could possibly have been taken amidst the endless plain of snow that surrounded them.

On 8 January, Shackleton records:

Again all day in our bags, suffering considerably physically from cold hands and feet, and from hunger, but more mentally, for we cannot get on south, and we simply lie here shivering. Every now and then one of our party's feet go, and the unfortunate beggar has to take his leg out of the sleeping-bag and have his frozen foot nursed into life again by placing it inside the shirt, against the skin of his almost equally unfortunate neighbour. We must do something more to the south, even though the food is going, and we weaken lying in the cold, for with 72 deg of frost, the winds cut through our thin tent, and even the drift is finding its way in and on to our bags, which are wet enough as it is. Cramp is not uncommon every now and then, and the drift all around the tent has made it so small that there is hardly room for us all. The wind has been blowing hard all day; some of the gusts must be over seventy or eighty miles an hour. This evening it seems as though it were going to ease down, and directly it does we shall be up and away south for a rush. I feel that this march must be our limit. We are so short of food, and at this high altitude, 11,600 feet, it is hard to keep any warmth in our bodies between the scanty meals. We have nothing to read now, having depoted our books to save weight, and it is dreary work lying in the tent with nothing to read, and too cold to write much in the diary.

9 January was the expedition's last possible day to get as far as they could. Shackleton called the proposed planting of the flag their 'Furthest South'.

In the early hours of the morning the wind had eased, and at 4 a.m. they started south with the flag and a brass cylinder containing stamps and documents to be placed at the furthest point south they could reach. By nine, the expedition were like eager schoolboys, half running, half walking over a surface that had been hardened by the blizzard. They felt strange for they had no ponies and no sledge to drag along behind them.

Eventually they reached a spot where they hoisted the flag, and took possession of the plateau in the name of his Majesty. They looked south towards the pole with powerful binoculars, but could see nothing but the endless plain. They were all sure that, somewhere in that flat, barbaric wilderness lay the South Pole.

The expedition only stayed a few minutes; having eaten a frugal meal they hurried back, reaching their camp by about 3 p.m. Exhausted they marched for another two hours in the afternoon and pitched camp at 5.30 p.m.

Fortunately their tracks were still visible in the snow, and Shackleton and his men were able to follow them back to the sea. The long journey was made even more difficult by the knowledge that they had failed, and yet the four men were further away from civilization than any human being before them.

'Whatever regrets may be, we have done our best,' wrote Shackleton stoically. They were lucky to be alive.

Terry Waite survived an incredible 1,763 days – just under four years – in solitary confinement in Beirut. His methods of dealing with isolation for such a length of time were remarkable, and showed how deep the inner resources of a human being can be.

For most of his period of solitary confinement, Waite had no writing materials, no news of the outside world and, for a long while, no books. As a result, he 'wrote' his autobiography in his head, returning to his earliest memories and progressing through them at a measured rate, trying not to use up too many at a time, not knowing how long he would have to endure captivity.

Waite's family had no idea whether he was alive or dead. Neither did anyone else. Thinking of them was such a horrifyingly painful process that he was forced to retreat into his memories to keep himself sane.

'But even these,' he said, 'can be too painful to relive, and there were also considerable holes in my ability to recall some events. Curiously, for instance, I couldn't remember any details of my kidnap at all, and though I racked my brains nothing about it would come back to me. It was only later I remembered how I came to be abducted, and then I couldn't think why on earth I hadn't been able to recall the details earlier. I suppose it was shock.'

For the majority of his confinement, Waite was chained in a variety of different hiding places, most of which were squalid, bleak and miserably uncomfortable. He rarely saw daylight. He was either freezing cold or boiling hot, had to put on a blindfold whenever his captors brought him food or wished to interrogate him, and, towards the end, almost died through bouts of infection, asthma and bronchitis which were only occasionally treated.

Shortly after capture he was taken by van, blindfolded, to a garage in Beirut. Below a trapdoor was a nine-foot drop to an underground room. Still blindfolded, Waite was forced to jump down to an earth floor and led across to a door. Once inside he found himself in *'an empty cell lined with white tiles. I sat down on the floor and looked around. The room was almost seven feet across and about ten feet long. The height varied between six feet and six feet nine. I could be certain about that because I am six feet seven inches tall and in places it was impossible to stand upright. A heavy steel door with several thick iron bars on top secured the entrance. Cautiously, I looked through. There were a number of cells in this underground prison in which dim light burned. I assumed they were occupied. I had heard of the underground prisons of Beirut ... There were stories about prisoners*

*being incarcerated for years in such places. I sat
down again and began to prepare myself for an
ordeal. First I would strengthen my will by fast-
ing; I would refuse all food for at least a week.
Second, I would make three resolutions to support
me through whatever was to come: no regrets, no
sentimentality, no self-pity. Then I did what gen-
erations of prisoners have done before me. I stood
up and, bending my head, I began to walk round
and round and round and round.'*

Despite all the despair and the appalling hardship that was to follow, Terry Waite never lost
sight of his resolutions.

By the mid-eighties hostage-taking as a political
weapon had become an epidemic, especially in
the Middle East. As the Archbishop's Special
Envoy, Terry Waite had used his charismatic
diplomatic skills to negotiate the release of
hostages in Iran and Libya. It was only when he
came to focus on the release of the American
hostages in the Lebanese Civil War that questions began to be asked in the media. Had Waite
been misunderstood? Had he plunged from the
public view of a man of God, objective and
unpolitical, to someone who could well have been
manipulated by the United States government –
in particular by the dubious influence of Colonel

Oliver North, born-again Christian, American nationalist and Deputy Assistant Director for Political-Military Affairs on the National Security Council staff?

One of North's tasks was to liaise with the families of American hostages in the Middle East. He had considerably increased that role, however, to assume operational control to free the Lebanese hostages. Mindful of his country's loss of face in Vietnam, North was determined that he would restore America's sense of national pride and identity. He must have seen Terry Waite as a godsend, and allegedly seized the opportunity to use him as a pawn for the Reagan administration.

Since being publicly disgraced, following the Iran-Contra enquiry, at that time North was in fact secretly trading arms with Middle Eastern countries in return for the release of the American hostages, while Terry Waite negotiated on behalf of the Archbishop of Canterbury.

Waite denies any knowledge of the arms trading. 'There are plenty of Norths around,' he told me. 'Professional negotiators acting on behalf of politicians. I was acting on behalf of the Church and would never have agreed to the arms trading – either as the Archbishop's envoy or as an individual.'

Although Waite says he had no knowledge of

North's activities or the risks he ran by associating with him, his known contact with North placed Waite in considerable danger. By the time he made his final trip to Beirut the arms deal had broken down and there is little doubt that this is why Waite was swiftly taken hostage himself.

However, Waite told me: 'If I had been seen as a double dealer I would soon have been killed.' But after interrogation (and torture), it became clear that Waite was what his captors had always assumed him to be – a Christian negotiator.

In the early eighties, Waite joined Lambeth Palace, the London home and office of Dr Runcie, then Archbishop of Canterbury. He was employed as Secretary for Anglican Communion Affairs.

The Anglican Church was strictly apolitical and Waite was originally responsible for organizing overseas visits for Dr Runcie. He had not been in the job long, however, when three British missionaries were arrested in Iran and accused of spying. This was at the beginning of the Islamic revolution and the rise to power of Ayatollah Khomeini.

Dr Runcie sent Terry Waite to Tehran, conscious that this was a religious matter and best resolved by the Church. If the Foreign Office intervened, then politics could only further undermine the position of the missionaries. Waite arrived in Tehran in December 1980, dressed in a long black cassock and wearing a cross, looking very much like a religious leader himself, his beard and apparel heightening the drama of his appearance.

Waite made his own position very clear. He was a representative of the Christian Church and had absolutely nothing to do with the British government. With other Anglicans he organized a service in St Paul's Church in Tehran, but as Waite began his sermon a small contingent of Revolutionary Guards burst in, armed with automatic weapons.

Waite strolled down the aisle, and in greeting the guards noted that one of them was carrying a tape recorder. He asked them to sit in the front row, the tape was switched on and Waite began his sermon again so that its content could be recorded for the Revolution.

As a result, Terry Waite made an extremely favourable impression and was allowed to visit the missionaries in prison. Months later, they were freed.

After the freeing of the Iran missionaries, Waite became a national hero and he was awarded the MBE. Gavin Hewitt, who produced a *Panorama* film about Waite's kidnapping, wrote in his book, *Terry Waite – Why was he kidnapped?*:

All the right ingredients were present. An ordinary individual, unaffected, unknown, had charmed Islamic Revolutionaries with common sense, integrity and a dash of humour. The media, in their endless quest for heroes, had found a candidate rich in solid British virtues.

Before he was kidnapped in Beirut, Waite went to the rescue of other hostages in Libya, and whilst negotiating their release was contacted by the Presbyterian Church in America in connection with Benjamin Weir, one of their ministers who was being held hostage in the Lebanon. This was the beginning of the end.

On 8 January, 1985, Martin Jenco, a Catholic priest, was taken hostage in Beirut and a few months later, Terry Anderson, who was chief Middle East correspondent for Associated Press, was also captured. Earlier, in 1984, William Buckley, CIA Station Chief in Lebanon, had also been kidnapped. Slowly, unwillingly, the Reagan administration began to realize they had another hostage crisis on their hands.

Assisted by the Director of the Episcopal Church's fund for disaster relief, Waite became involved as negotiator, and was put in touch with Oliver North, who was liaising with the hostage families.

As he had been held at arm's length by the State Department, Waite found North by contrast both caring and dynamic. North also had a cause to fight. He had served in Vietnam, won medals, been wounded and felt America had betrayed herself by withdrawing. His role, as he saw it, was to reassert America's image as a world power.

The suggestion that arms might well be traded for the US hostages came from Iranian contacts with the US government. To the CIA, this was an attractive idea, for they were terrified that if Ayatollah Khomeini died the communists might take over.

On 20 August, 100 anti-tank missiles were flown from Israel to Iran in the belief they were being swapped for the hostages. Unfortunately, the missiles ended up in the hands of an opposing faction. It was agreed that a further 408 missiles were to be sent in exchange for William Buckley. Inconveniently, he had already died.

Benjamin Weir and Father Martin Jenco were now being held in Beirut together. They later learnt that Terry Anderson was in the same building, as were David Jacobsen, administrator of the American University Hospital in Beirut, and Thomas Sutherland, Dean of the School of Agriculture. The hostages were increasing in number and soon were all being held together.

In the early summer of 1985, the Archbishop of Canterbury agreed that Waite should negotiate for the release of the American hostages and he began to prepare for his first trip to Beirut, a mission that was surrounded by high profile media attention. Negotiating with the captors of the US hostages who wanted Iranian prisoners freed from Kuwait, Waite was able to verify that the prisoners, with the exception of Buckley, were alive and in reasonably good health. He was to return several times, but still there was no sign of any release.

Meanwhile, Oliver North continued to plot trade-off deals. His plans were complex. In May of 1985, he had promised radar systems to Iran and hoped that as a result of this deal the Lebanese captors would release their hostages to the Iranian capital of Tehran. This, however, was still only a plan; North was not sure whether Iran and the Lebanon would even be able to agree amongst themselves. Waite, meanwhile, had been warned before his last visit to Beirut not to return. His contacts were now suspicious and his former objective integrity was thought to be seriously in question.

For his part, Waite considered himself to be 'liaising' with Oliver North and US Intelligence rather than working for them. The thin red line in between, however, was becoming blurred to the Lebanese hostage-takers, who had stressed that far from being gangsters, they were devout Muslims.

Eventually, the combined, if disparate endeavours of Oliver North and Terry Waite were successful in that one hostage – Father Martin Jenco – was at last set free.

In November 1986, the situation became more optimistic when David Jacobsen was released with a note from his captors which was hopeful yet threatening at the same time, emphasizing an intense hatred for America and underlining how dangerous Terry Waite's position was.

We announced to world opinion, to the American people, and to the families of the hostages the release of the American, David Jacobsen. We hold the American government responsible for the consequences of not benefiting from this opportunity by continuing what it, the American government, has begun, through proceeding with proposals that may lead, if continued, to the solution of the issue of the hostages. We remind the American government ... that we will follow an entirely different course in the event the American government does not complete these proposals in order to attain the desired result. We pledge to everyone that we will continue the Jihad [holy war] until the establishment of Allah's rule on earth, the destruction of idols and tyrants, and the victory of the oppressed and downtrodden. The Will of Allah be done. Islamic

Jihad Organization. November 1986.

This note was enough to make anyone realize how deeply the Americans were hated in the Middle East. If he had stayed neutral he would have been safe. Now, however, Waite, through no fault of his own, had lost the image of neutrality that had been his greatest strength.

Despite the fact that he was visibly shaken and had become wary instead of ebullient, he was still determined to press on with his rescue mission – somehow to obtain the release of Terry Anderson and Tom Sutherland. He was, however, increasingly aware of the Oliver North scandal and what was being called Irangate.

Unfortunately it was becoming increasingly obvious to Waite that the hostages released so far owed their return to the arms deal rather than his personal intervention. It was deeply galling for him, particularly when a London magazine headlined an article *'Was Terry Waite used as a pawn by the Reagan Administration?'*

North, meanwhile, well on his rake's progress, had been dismissed from the National Security Council. The Administration also declared to Tehran that they would not be giving any more arms to Iran, a statement that just preceded Waite's return to Beirut.

A few days before flying to Beirut, Waite said

that there was a *'high element of risk, when I leave all my security behind ... I'm entirely dependent on my reputation ... I am absolutely vulnerable.'*

He wanted to meet with the hostages' captors, returning to his original negotiating position as the representative of the Church. Within days he had been taken hostage himself.

'I think one reason for my kidnap might have been motivated by the Lebanese Hezbullah who had little liking for the Iranian intervention and might have seen me as a valuable negotiating tool,' he told me.

During his years of imprisonment, Waite was moved from one place to another, for the most part apartments in the city, always kept in squalid conditions and usually chained. He was either intolerably cold or so hot that he could hardly cope.

Eventually he was forced to give up his hunger strike, resigning himself to face a long ordeal. Fortunately, however, Waite had considerable mental reserves, and he created for himself an inner life that made him just able to withstand the horrors of a situation that might, in fact, last for ever. By no means the least of the tortures he had to endure was the realization that without natural light, his wristwatch confiscated, Waite could only guess at the interminable passing of the days.

Because of his resources, he was able to take mental journeys, which he so movingly describes in *Taken On Trust*.

I return to my bed, fold my blanket and sit cross-legged on the floor. I want to pray. The words of the Communion service from the Book of Common Prayer come to mind. I find that I remember most of the service. When I come to the consecration of the bread and wine, as I have neither, I use my imagination and go back to a church I have known in the past – St Bartholomew's, Wilmslow, the church in which I was confirmed. I am sitting with people I love. Tomorrow I will imagine myself among friends at the Russian Orthodox Church in Kensington.

During the first few days in his underground prison, Waite was given food and was allowed one visit a day to the toilet. He had also been given a bottle in which to urinate and was instructed to whisper to his guards when they arrived in his cell. He was also compelled to put on a blindfold immediately they knocked on his door and keep it on until he was alone again.

Without books or any kind of reading material, Waite decided to exercise, pacing his cell, counting each pace, mentally assessing the miles that he was building up. After some miles he lapsed into a trance-like state, as if his body had settled down into its own rhythm. At the front of his mind he counted, and behind it he drifted into long reminiscences. Later he would question himself. How long could he survive down here? How long could he tolerate being alone? Waite had heard of priests in China surviving twenty years or more in solitary confinement. To achieve whatever length of time was necessary, he knew he would have to keep mentally and spiritually healthy. Then Waite lay back on his mattress and returned to his childhood and to the deliberately slow unwinding of his past.

Despite these abilities to take journeys into the memory, Waite was all too well aware that he had given specific instruction for his life *not* to be bargained for by the authorities and that all his captors' demands should be refused. He also knew that his instructions would be obeyed; a deeply depressing thought.

Waite told me he 'tried to do everything I could to avoid depression, the feeling of darkness falling.' He wrote his autobiography in his mind and remembered that Jung had said that if only the individual would allow it, the unconscious part of the mind would come to his aid. 'We all have to remember that the measurement of time is cultural conditioning.' To Waite, the days became circular, time began to bend. 'You can reach an accommodation with solitude,' he said. 'Grow towards it by choice. But I had no choice so I was compelled to seek it out. Solitude is not loneliness; there is a substantial difference.'

When I asked Waite if he could ever forgive his guards, he replied without hesitation, 'Yes, of course I can. They were either blindly loyal followers or psychopaths. Either way they had lived in appalling conditions and saw the West as rich and uncaring.'

His most pressing and ever present terror was that he was going to be tortured. Still in his underground cell, Waite had already wondered why it was tiled. Then, slowly, he became convinced that the tiles made the cells easier to clean up after the torturing of their prisoners – a nightmare that stayed with him for some time. Never had he felt so alone.

The long flights, the endless press conferences and meetings already seemed years away. For one who had so rarely been alone, now Waite had his own company twenty-four hours a day. This was only alleviated by his guards, whom he could not see, could only whisper to and who rarely spoke to him when they arrived with inadequate food or grudgingly to take him on his much needed once a day trip to the toilet.

At home in England, Waite had a wife, Frances, and four children. He did not dare, however, to think too much about them, for if he did, he knew he would weaken, break down and not be able to survive an ordeal whose length he could not possibly imagine. Could he hope to be released in days? In weeks? Or was he going to have to force himself to think more long term? Would he be forgotten? Would the UK and the USA take him at his word and make no attempt to rescue him? Yet he had meant what he had said.

He also tried many different methods of survival, such as counting the white tiles which lined his cell. When that task was over, he would attempt mental arithmetic. Waite's father had been good with numbers, and when his son was three he would encourage him to add up the numbers on car licence plates.

Some days later, still confused, Waite was removed to another hiding place. There, his interrogators insisted that he write, in detail, the story of his life, but as he had left his reading glasses behind in the hotel, Waite was asked to dictate his autobiography instead.

He dictated for an hour until his scribe became too exhausted to continue. Eventually a video camera arrived and Waite was forced to tell the story again. Back in his chains, Terry Waite realized that the video tapes could easily be edited.

Some time later, the television was turned up to full volume and a couple of pillows were placed over Waite's head while one of his captors sat on them. Then another removed the blanket covering his legs and he was beaten on the soles of his feet with what he thought was a cable.

The beating stopped after an agonizing dozen strokes and his persecutor ran his finger down the length of Waite's foot to see if there was any feeling left. There was and the beating resumed. When it was finished, Waite was asked to tell his captors what he knew. He quietly replied that he knew nothing.

Later, having hardly recovered from the beating, Waite was told he had five hours to live. He was then left alone in his room. After a while his tormentors returned and he was told that he had been sentenced to death by Muslim law and that he could only write one letter.

His chains were removed and he was handed a biro and a writing pad. Ludicrously and barbarically, he was instructed not to remove his blindfold. Somehow looking underneath it, Terry Waite wrote the following which was addressed to the Archbishop, his family, his mother and various relatives and close friends:

This is the last letter I shall write. I have been told that I have a short time to live and that I can send this message to you. I am sorry that my life is ending in this way. I am not afraid to die, but I don't want to die without you knowing that I am well and in good spirits. Try not to be too sad. I have done my best and can die with a clear conscience. Also try not to be bitter against my captors. They have suffered much in their lives. I love you all.

God bless and goodbye. Terry.

Waite was not, however, to be executed; the threat was a bluff. He was much more use to his captors alive than dead, and although they continued to torture him mentally, telling him that his execution had only been postponed, he soon realized that the postponement was indefinite.

Solitary confinement continued and Waite did his mental and physical best to survive the ordeal. 'I couldn't communicate with the guards except on the most superficial of terms as their bosses would not have allowed debate,' he told me. Nevertheless, Waite soon reminded them that Muslim law held that it was wrong to steal. So why had they stolen him and the other hostages? 'I curled up at night in the foetal position,' he added. 'That's the most comfortable if you are chained.' He also continued to pray, not for himself but in the form of the Communion service.

When Waite was transferred to another safe house, farce intervened; he was dressed as an Islamic woman, looking rather larger than life at six foot seven. Here, the conditions were much worse. The room was damp and cold, and although there were, as yet, no staples for his chains, all Waite had to wear were socks, trousers and a shirt. The room originally had French windows but they had been removed and the gap covered by sheet metal. A single light bulb hung in the centre of the room and there was a small amount of graffiti scribbled on one wall.

Waite derived a great deal of comfort from the

graffiti, immediately feeling close to the anonymous earlier prisoner. To his surprise, he was unexpectedly given an electric fire and, even more surprisingly, an iron. Self-respect returned as he was able to dry out his mattress and iron his tattered trousers.

However, he had now contracted a skin condition and his face was badly swollen. His eyes were also considerably irritated, and one of his guards gave Waite a small bowl of olive oil so he could bathe them. Although the primitive medication made no difference, the incident proved that at least some of his captors were humane.

When he received a mattress, it was tied with a piece of raffia and he plaited this into the shape of a cross and hung it on the wall. Waite wrote: *This symbol of suffering and hope gives me a focus in my drab prison.*

His guards, deeply religious themselves, did not take it down and the cross remained, perhaps also symbolizing the purity of Waite's original mission. To his continual requests for books there was no response at all, although eventually, after a long delay, medicine was provided.

Gradually Terry Waite created a specific routine for himself and to keep to it each day became an obsession, rightly so because its framework promoted his mental health.

He woke early and said his prayers. Then he

would exercise and eat a breakfast of bread and occasionally a few olives. Afterwards, the whole day lay ahead like a vast and unexplored sea. He was learning to be quiet and still within, as calm as he could be in the circumstances, but he didn't want too much stillness, for inner tension was required to keep his mind alive. He continued to forage for memories of his childhood and teenage years. Slowly Waite began to recall the names of people he had not seen in years. The memory drawers were opening, working to help him survive the long, barren days of captivity.

Completely out of the blue, Waite suddenly received a present that entirely altered his prison existence. One of his guards gave him a book: *Beyond Euphrates* by Freya Stark. First of all he held it to his face to capture the wonderful lingering smell of a new book. It immediately took him back to his childhood and the sensuous smell of new volumes in the local bookshop. Then he checked to see how many pages there were. The next stage was to count the words on each page so that he would know exactly how long it would take him to read the book. He told himself he would savour each morsel of prose, but at the same time knew he didn't have enough strength for such an act of self-denial.

His guards also gave Waite a small plastic magnifying glass as a substitute for his reading glasses. Later, as the heat grew more fierce, he was given a ventilation fan. Although Waite was grateful for its appearance, it was also an indication that his captors planned to keep him imprisoned for some time.

The uncharted days passed until he could not remember how long he had been held.

He was moved again, this time to much better conditions in part of a flat that belonged to a young couple. His foot was chained to a radiator but he received his breakfast on a plastic tray. He still had to put on his blindfold before anyone entered the room, so Waite stood no chance of identifying his captors or getting a glimpse of someone who was perhaps more humane. The food was certainly better, though, and after his meal a television set was wheeled into the room. Ironically, he watched *The Benny Hill Show* with Arabic subtitles. What he really wanted to watch was the news, but this was forbidden. However, one of his guards did tell him that he had been shortlisted for the Nobel Prize.

More books were produced and Waite continued to exercise. The better food and living conditions improved his health, but this more promising situation was not to last.

First of all, the chain round his leg was reinstalled. Then, to Waite's disappointment, he was moved again, to a building in Beirut where three sets of metal staples had been driven into the walls. Clearly other prisoners had been held here before him. To be back in such conditions deeply depressed him, and although he was sure there was another prisoner on the same floor he could find no way of contacting him. His almost ghostly presence was underlined by the fact that the guards were now stepping up efforts to keep Waite quiet and this raised his curiosity unbearably.

Despite the return to basic conditions, he was eventually given a book again, and to his joy Waite discovered it was *The First Circle* by Alexander Solzhenitsyn.

By now he had noticed a shift in his relationship with his captors. The initial suspicion and hostility had disappeared, and Waite was now being treated as half-guest, half-prisoner. He was allowed the luxury of taking a shower each morning, he was given a haircut and antibiotics to stop an infection in his ear.

Waite also received a small portable TV to watch in the evenings, but the moment the news was broadcast, a guard arrived to remove the set, a habit that was as annoying as it was regular.

Waite, however, decided on an ingenious plan to beat the guards at their robotic game and have a glimpse of what was happening in the outside world.

Just before the news bulletin, and the time of the guard's arrival, Waite would switch off the set. Gradually he got the guard used to the routine until one night he arrived in his room, saw the set dutifully turned off and closed the door without removing it. Trying to catch Waite out, the guard wrenched open the door and checked on him, but Waite was sitting with his back against the wall at a reasonable distance from the TV set. The dramatic and farcical reappearances continued for some time until the guard slowly became convinced that Waite had no intention of turning on the set himself.

Waite delayed for a further week before putting his master plan into operation, which was to turn the brightness down together with the volume and then put his ear to the loudspeaker on the side of the set. The trick was to have one hand on the on/off switch, his ear to the loudspeaker and eyes firmly fixed on the crack beneath the door.

As a result, he heard at least local news in English. Whenever he saw a shadow under the door, he would flick off the switch and get into an innocent sitting position just as the door burst open.

Despite the absurd nature of this game, Waite was extremely tense as he knew he would be severely punished if discovered listening.

His guards, however, were still suspicious and told him they had installed a small transmitter microphone. They claimed they knew he was listening and promised he would be in big trouble. The set was taken away, but the big trouble never happened. Instead, a cardboard box arrived which Waite later discovered was full of books that were supposed to be allocated to him, one at a time, by his guards.

Some months later, he even received a postcard showing a stained glass window with John Bunyan sitting at a table and gazing through the bars of his cell in Bedford jail. The address had been obliterated and the postmark was blurred so Waite had no means of identifying how it had reached him. The card read:

Dear Terry
You are not forgotten. People everywhere are praying for your release, and that of the other hostages.
With best wishes,
Joy Brodier

He had no idea who Joy Brodier was, but this first contact from the outside world brought Terry Waite comfort beyond description. Once again, time passed until two other prisoners arrived and were placed in the next room.

Eventually one of them contacted him by tapping out an alphabet code which in the end Waite understood.

ABCDEFGHIJ. Then a pause.

ABCDEFGHIJKLMNO. Another pause.

ABCDEFGH. Waite realized the hostage was tapping out his name. John. John McCarthy.

Soon he was moved again, this time to a smaller room, but there was no metal sheeting over the French window. The light and fresh air, however, were not to last for long. As the sound of people approaching the room was heard, Terry Waite automatically slipped his blindfold over his eyes. Then he heard an electric drill and in mounting despair knew exactly what was happening. Later, when the workmen had gone, he was able to take off his blindfold and see for himself what he had dreaded so much. All too familiar metal sheets covered the French window.

Nevertheless, Waite still forced himself to re-explore the past, now being used up at an alarming rate however slowly he reimagined it all, and when this didn't work he continued to write his book in his head. As his health deteriorated, Waite tried to stiffen his mental resolve to survive. This was greatly helped when he slowly realized there were now three hostages imprisoned next door to him.

Eventually the alphabet code tapping signal

told him who they were: Terry Anderson, Tom Sutherland and John McCarthy.

At last. I've found you, tapped back Waite.

From them, he learnt that his family was well, that Brian Keenan (another hostage) had been released and both Waite's cousin and brother had been heard speaking on the World Service.

The other three hostages, obviously not considered as politically 'sensitive' as Terry Waite, had long had more privileges; they were able to listen to the BBC World Service, Radio Monte Carlo, the Voice of America, as well as local radio. As a result, they were very well informed and Terry Anderson spent hours tapping messages on to the wall to bring Waite fully up to date.

Once again, Waite's guards relaxed and allowed him a small black and white television. Amazingly, they told him he could watch the news. He was also allowed to listen to the radio which he preferred, finding it more stimulating to his imagination.

One day, the guards entered his room and, to Waite's horror, began to pack up his scanty belongings. He wondered with great foreboding if he was being moved away from the others, losing privileges again, the thought of which was particularly distressing when he was in such failing health.

Instead, the guards walked him up the passage

a few paces, into the room where McCarthy, Anderson and Sutherland were held. They welcomed him warmly but Waite, in a state of shock, had very mixed feelings. He had now been in solitary for well over three years, and to be so suddenly catapulted into the company of others, however friendly they were, was disorientating and deeply inhibiting.

I had become accustomed to the room in which I was kept. Waite's admission is revealing. Despite his indomitable spirit, he had become psychologically dependent on his routine and his various ingenious methods of getting through the time without mental collapse. He had made himself an island and now it was invaded.

'But in another way,' he told me, 'I was glad to have the company and more easily hear news of the outside world. But if you and I were kept chained in an extremely small room, we would soon come to pick up changes of mood, highs and lows. The other hostages must have realized the irony of the situation. I had come to help them, to try and negotiate their release, but now was imprisoned with them. What was more, these hostages had been together a long time and each had established his own emotional space. I was the new boy and had to find out how to live alongside them.'

Inevitably there were difficulties of adjustment. Waite had picked up a virus while in solitary, and having joined the others his breathing became worse and he would sit up all night in a chair wheezing heavily, realizing how disruptive this must be to the others' sleep.

Terry Anderson was quick to intervene on behalf of Waite's health and eventually he was taken to a doctor who prescribed a ventalin inhaler for his asthma. This made a considerable difference; he was at last able to cope with his breathing difficulties and the paroxysms of coughing.

John McCarthy was the first to be released and then, to their numbed disbelief, Terry Waite and Tom Sutherland were released together, followed by Terry Anderson – all eventually handed over to Syrian Intelligence.

The appalling ordeal was over and Waite was returned to his family. Like other hostages, however, he had considerable difficulty in adapting to normal life and he wrote: *One part of me longs for the solitary life, longs to go into the desert with my books and papers and devote myself entirely to the interior journey. Another part recognizes that I must find a balance. A balance between family, solitude and community.*

CHAPTER 4

RANULPH FIENNES' LONG WALK

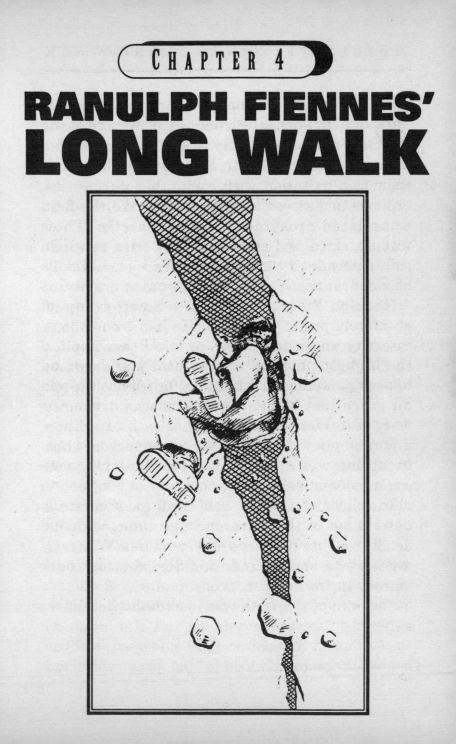

Sir Ranulph Fiennes, explorer and author, and Dr Michael Stroud, explorer and medical doctor, not only beat the savage elements to reach the South Pole but they also beat their own irritation with each other during this arduous and stressful attempt to make the first unassisted crossing of the Antarctic. They walked, skied and experimentally tried to windsail, determined that the long walk should only be aided *naturally*, either from wind or gravity.

Ranulph Fiennes is one of a small group of absolutely purist explorers. He has tremendous integrity and a toughness of mind that applies the highest physical and mental standards to himself as well as to others. As for friendship - on an expedition of this nature he was distinctly wary of it. Fiennes believed that each expedition member must look out for themselves, that friendship was a plus factor, not something you could automatically count on.

The cliché of a 'white hell' is all too accurate a description of the Antarctic continent, with its deadly cold, its blizzards and crevasses. Winter is much worse and Fiennes and Stroud spent their journey racing against its onset.

The pain of the walk was incredible. Both men suffered from snowblindness and starvation as they dragged 500-pound (200 kilogram) sledges behind them. In addition to this, they contracted severe pressure sores and gangrene as well as almost dying from hypothermia. The fact that Stroud was a doctor and had brought with him antibiotics and other medication certainly saved their lives. Although Stroud was younger and fitter and stronger than Fiennes, all these advantages were diminished by Fiennes's amazing willpower which drove him on beyond the limits of human endurance. He was inspired by a number of former Antarctic explorers, in particular Amundsen, Scott, Shackleton, Fuchs and Swan. It was Swan who provided the most emotive encouragement.

(South Pole, 1986)

The Pole will unshackle me from the awful fear of failure and the burden of having to win at all costs. I have to feel that life is worthwhile. If or when we pull this [the South Pole] *off, I will have done something extraordinary which will give me the opportunity I long for.*

I hate living in a stinking tent with other men. I hate being cold and you must be a pervert to like having ice inside your underpants. Someone said it was the cleanest and most isolated way of having a bad time ever devised ... But it pumps up your ego ... There is a side of me that wouldn't mind dying out there. In fact I would quite like it in a way."

Born in 1944, Ranulph Fiennes was educated at Eton and commissioned into the Royal Scots Greys in 1963, and attached to 22 SAS Regiment in 1966. Since then he has led several major expeditions, including the three-year Transglobe Expedition. He was awarded an honorary doctorate of science by Loughborough University; he has also received the Founder's Medal of the Royal Geographical Society and the Polar Medal with Bar from the Queen.

Fiennes saw Antarctica as a huge wedding cake covered by glutinous icing that was slowly flowing outwards and downwards. Most of the bases were built along the shore and the interior was wild and treacherous. In 1979, however, he had been part of a previous Antarctic crossing, so he knew what to expect. The only difference – and it was a substantial one – was that this current expedition was on foot and was therefore going to be dramatically much harder. Nevertheless, even Fiennes experience and planning could never reveal just how dreadful conditions were going to be.

Even at an early stage, when both men were still fit, the most testing incidents occurred, almost as a taster of what might follow. The crevasses, largely invisible, soon presented a major problem and, sharing the navigation, Fiennes and Stroud were on a flat stretch with no tell-tale sign of undulations when Fiennes found himself falling. He writes:

I flung both arms out, ski-sticks flailing. My descent stopped short at my armpits. I felt my legs involuntarily treading air, swimming on the void. Gingerly I tried to turn my neck to look backwards at the sledge. My greatest fear at that moment was that it too would break through the thin trap-door and, like Ninnis, I would cartwheel downwards to snap my spine or crack open my skull on some sharp icy ledge below.

Made virtually blind by breathing into his goggles as he fell, the resultant mist turning to ice, Fiennes realized that any undue movement of his body could collapse the snow bridge below him and make him fall further into the abyss below. If this happened, Fiennes knew he would not emerge alive. He couldn't see his sledge because the hood of his parka and his cotton balaclava prevented any lateral movement of his neck.

Nevertheless, he managed to wriggle his way out, crawling to one side of the crater and hauling the sledge from its immediate vicinity.

Later that day, Michael Stroud disappeared from view and Fiennes looked up at his despairing shout. There followed the sound of rushing air and snow thundering from the bridge beneath him as it collapsed. Fiennes was about 500 yards away and could now see nothing but Stroud's head, a dark shape against the snow. Then he saw the alloy manhaul poles and the sledge itself.

The crevasse was only six feet (2 metres) in width, but sheer sides had opened up beneath both Stroud and his sledge. His hips were across the far lip and his arms were reaching out desperately for a grip, but his alloy traces prevented Stroud from moving in any direction because the sledge was poised for half its length over the chasm.

Fiennes tore himself clear of the harness he had been using to haul his own sledge and grabbed the back of Stroud's to try and stop it moving forwards. If Fiennes had allowed the sledge to slide into the crevasse, Stroud would have been pulled back from his balancing point and plunged down with it.

To prevent this happening, Fiennes proceeded to push the sledge towards Stroud, enabling him to crawl as far forward as the traces of his harness would allow so that he could free himself in case the sledge plunged into the crevasse. He managed to unclip his harness and extricate himself. Then, between them, Fiennes and Stroud stood either side of the drop. Applying as much force as they could, Fiennes pushed and Stroud pulled until Stroud fell backwards and dragged the 480-pound (200 kilo) sledge over the far lip of the fissure.

Ranulph Fiennes is a remarkable writer as well as a remarkable explorer, and his description of the forces in Antarctica is highly evocative:

That night the ice beneath and around us pushed on towards the sea as it had for millennia. Sometimes a giant boulder, house high, is torn from an inland nunatak and transported on ice for hundreds of miles to the nearest coast; then out over vast ice shelves until at length it floats to sea on an iceberg. Sometimes the ice beneath the boulder will melt above *the sea's surface but, for many weeks, continue to float above the southern ocean with only its rocky burden visible to awestruck passing sailors.*

The same night Stroud wrote in his diary: *'Towards the end of the day I felt desperately tired*

*and arrived at the tent ten minutes after Ran,
sick with fatigue. I felt quite dazed and cold ...
Ran also felt it was one of his "hardest days
ever".*

But worse, much worse, was to come, particularly as sores and abscesses became a common ailment with both men. At one point, Stroud (or Dr Stroud as he called himself when carrying out medical tests on Fiennes or himself), decided to operate on a swollen abscess on his heel. He gave himself two deep injections of xylocaine anaesthetic and then plunged his scalpel deep into the swelling and began to make incisions. While Fiennes looked on warily as pus poured from the wound, Stroud then bandaged his foot and calmly put away his medical equipment. Fiennes was feeling faint by this stage. Blisters and what he calls crotch rot were other daily hazards, and soon plasters were in dangerously short supply.

Although they were both eating 5,200 calories a day, a third of the way into the journey Fiennes had lost twenty pounds (nine kilos) and Stroud had lost fifteen (seven), but despite all these problems both men were still determined not to nit-pick at each other or lose their tempers. Irritating personal mannerisms just had to be tolerated.

Gradually, however, mutual irritation did begin to break out, particularly when Stroud contracted severe diarrhoea and had to keep stopping. His diary read: *I began to feel ill early and got diarrhoea after two and a half hours. Ran is unsympathetic, angry and a right sod.*

Fiennes was desperately concerned about the time-frame of the expedition, but his short temper only made Stroud sourly miserable and after more delays (and diarrhoea) Fiennes apologized and the atmosphere lightened.

On the fifty-eighth day of the expedition, both men were exhausted. They had now been trekking for such a long time that they felt they had known no other existence. What lay ahead – another fifty or sixty days – was distinctly untenable. Their performances were sure to degenerate. Stroud confided to his diary that he was finding it very difficult to keep going.

Over the last two hundred miles to the Pole it was necessary to climb 10,000 feet. Fiennes and Stroud were now on their sixty-seventh day and the South Pole was only fifteen miles away, but the wind chill factor was -84° C, with an accompanying thick fog. Later, stopping to relieve himself, Stroud made a near fatal error by taking his hands out of his mittens which were made of special oiled wool. Standing beside him, his already swollen feet as painful as at any time he could remember, Fiennes could hear him sobbing with pain and fear, his fingers starting to become frost-bitten as he tried to force his hands back into mittens that were too tight. Realizing that Stroud would lose his fingers completely if he didn't help him, Fiennes yelled at him to put his hands inside his trousers. This was the only way he was able to warm his hands up sufficiently so at least some of the blood circulation returned. But this was not a total remedy and five of his fingers had already become frost-bitten in that very short space of time.

The shock had been great and contributed to Stroud's hypothermia, which was exhibited in a particularly startling and unsettling way.

Because Stroud wouldn't reply to him and was standing, staring vacantly ahead, his head slightly lolling, Fiennes rapidly erected the tent and returned to find his companion kneeling in the snow and staring fixedly at nothing at all. Dragging him into the tent, Fiennes noticed Stroud's movements were wooden and jerky, and although he drank a cup of soup he still said nothing. He slept for a while and then woke, staring up at the ceiling, clearly unable to remember what had happened.

Stroud recovered, and later they staggered on towards the South Pole. At 7p.m., Fiennes topped a small rise and afterwards thought he saw a movement. Removing his goggles and trying to focus his eyes, he could just make out a series of blurred objects that closely resembled half a dozen black marbles dancing on the shimmer of the southern horizon.

He turned back and yelled to Stroud. Fiennes was actually gazing at the Pole. It was a rare moment of sheer elation. Although the journey was far from over he knew they had enough stores on the sledges to allow them to cross the continent and survive – if their luck held.

Once beyond the Pole, they both discovered that the Antarctic could actually become colder. Stroud wrote on the seventy-third day of the expedition: *'A desperately cold day, perhaps –40 ° C, with a stiff wind that kept us deeply chilled despite wearing all our clothing and going as best we could. My hands were very bad and, after each pee, they took thirty minutes to recover. Even then they would still be weak which led to further problems at the next pee – a vicious circle.'*

Stroud's morale, however, had much improved, particularly as they were well over half way now. Fiennes had calculated that if they continued at this pace and received no help from the wind, they should make the glacier top in a further seventeen days. Stroud was sure he could last.

Meanwhile, Fiennes' foot, already badly infected, had become much worse and Stroud diagnosed *'deep-seated infection in the foot-bone.'* He was able to prescribe antibiotics but they were now running out of the most effective ones. What with this, their increasing fatigue and the penetrating cold, both felt like giving up. Somehow they managed to press on.

Fiennes and Stroud were soon rewarded by the sight of a mountain range, tangible evidence of progress, and realized that at last they would be leaving the grinding cold of the high plateau – although that meant descending a good 9,000-foot (3000 metre) labyrinth of ice and coping with the appalling dangers this area presented.

Gradually the Otway Massif and the peaks of distant mountains, the Transantarctic Range, came into view. This massive obstruction dammed a mile-deep ocean of ice, and was 2,000 miles long, 200 miles wide.

This moving sea of inland ice descended from the polar plateau, coming hard up against the upper flanks of the Transantarctic range. Even the 6,000-foot (2000 metre)-high peaks seemed vulnerable to the force of ice which had already drowned two-thirds of their rock mass. It was a titanic struggle of the elements.

Many thousands of great glaciers had already forced their way through this range, tearing down the sides of mountains, burying everything in their wake.

Climbing down the blue-ice was incredibly difficult. First they went down the wrong tributary and the wrong side of Mount Ward, but not too much of the vital schedule was lost. Fiennes and Stroud finally camped close to the Swithinbank route, having rounded Mount Ward and crossed a moraine to join a bigger tributary. In fact they later discovered they had achieved two days' journey in one. Although this was consoling, the trek had now become a race against time – a race against the coming of winter when survival would be impossible. What was more, the rations were running out, and both men were now beginning to realize that they might have to give up.

Next day they switched to half-rations and both were walking in considerable pain.

Moving through the ice, its crevasse bridges and cliffs, was extremely testing, particularly with the sores and blisters that made their journey so horrendously painful. They both dreaded pulling their clothes on each morning. Despite his earlier problems, however, Stroud was in much better shape than Fiennes, to whom the putting on of a boot over his injured foot each morning was an agonizing process he anticipated grimly all night.

As they moved through the crevasse field, Fiennes and Stroud roped themselves together, the rope often spanning deep holes below them. When Fiennes moved too fast, Stroud yelled at him so he could keep the rope manoeuvrable but taut between them. When the surface was flat enough they also used the sails, some of the time making good progress.

Soon they sailed through a no man's land between the snow-capped mountains of the Commonwealth Range and the high walls of the Queen Alexandra massif. Fortunately, the 8,000-foot (2500-metre) high ramparts of the Cloudmaker were, for once, clear of mist, and for three hours they felt merely chilled instead of unbearably cold. To their immediate west lay an area through which some of Scott's men 'tumbled into the horrible pressure above the Cloudmaker.'

The wind took them too far east until, after an hour of traversing well-drifted fissures, a sudden katabatic struck from the south-east. Within seconds they were almost flown towards the distant ice cliffs of the Siege Dome. Both men clung to the sail line with one hand and the sledge ropes behind with the other. Bending their knees better to absorb the nasty shocks of ribbed ice, they sped on, fifty degrees off-course.

Although Fiennes and Stroud feared disaster, nothing happened, and as they crossed the glacier hunger began to dominate pain and fear. Fiennes found himself so ravenous that he was unable to conserve his two small bars of chocolate, calculated to last him all day. He couldn't concentrate on walking, navigation or anything else without thoughts of the succulence of the chocolate assuming a mythological state of importance in his mind. Eventually, it became an obsession, and to end the mental agony Fiennes decided to sit down and eat all the chocolate at once, which meant that he had consumed both bars virtually at the start of the day's journey. It was better to do this, he reasoned, than torture himself to such an extent.

Stroud was beginning to feel hypoglycaemic in the afternoon, a state not helped by having eaten two-thirds of his chocolate supply in the morning. He wondered how they would both feel after the food rations were further reduced.

Yet they still carried on, knowing that an airlift out would be cripplingly expensive. Besides, they had already made the singular achievement of having walked and skied and sailed hundreds of miles further than any of their unsupported predecessors – including Scott. Because of this, their spirits – so cast down before – were mounting, despite the obsessive hunger.

They again took stock of their rations and fuel, and reckoned it would last for ten days. The blizzard season was imminent, however, during which even a single storm can stop all travel, whether on foot or by air, for two or even three weeks without a break. It was an appalling prospect. They still had 360 miles on the Ross Ice-shelf to go before they would have a sighting of the ship and their chances of survival were becoming slim indeed. Fiennes knew they would be sensible to stop now and radio for help. Only one thing prevented him taking that decision. He wrote: *'Manhauling out on the ice-shelf was an unknown factor when applied to our current state. Until we tried it, we could not accurately summarize our remaining chances of reaching the ship and, from my point of view, avoiding possible bankruptcy.'*

On the ninety-fifth day of the expedition, amazingly still alive, Fiennes and Stroud were up against the onset of winter. In five days' time, their ship would be forced to leave the Ross Sea – and they still had 289 nautical miles to go to reach her. There was no wind so they couldn't sail, and they would need to achieve fifty-eight miles each day to ensure they caught the ship. At the moment they were barely covering twelve miles a day. Fiennes finally decided to call a halt to the expedition. Surely they had achieved enough, particularly for the multiple sclerosis sufferers for whom they were sponsored by the mile.

Whether or not the London insurers would pay out for the airlift depended on the two men's state of health, but there was little doubt that it was dramatically poor. Fortunately, the weather held and the twin Otter ski-plane that had dropped them off on the Atlantic coast came to pick them up from the Pacific coast.

Once in the plane, Fiennes and Stroud discovered the true extent of their bodily weaknesses. Their legs had become swollen, they were unable to focus their vision, they were barely able to rise from a prone position and they felt sick, giddy and disorientated. Neither man could possibly have carried on.

Fiennes concluded: *'I am no philosopher. I do agree with Murray, but I would add that a great deal of luck (or, if you are religious, help from above) is also involved. The frozen continent that we crossed is, after all, ruled by the untamed might of Nature. A single storm could have wiped us out, mind over matter notwithstanding, but Antarctica suffered our passing as a giant that allows a fly to crawl across his face."*

CHAPTER 5

SARAJEVO UNDER SIEGE

'*Imagine, one day you are sitting in London,*' a Serb friend who had remained in Sarajevo and fought for the Bosnians, told Janine di Giovanni, '*and the barricades go up, and you start getting attacked by the Welsh, or the Scots. Imagine that suddenly your water is turned off, your electricity, and your brothers, your father,*'

your boyfriend are sent off to the front line to become snipers. They don't come back. Your city is destroyed, and Europe looks on and does nothing. What would happen to you inside?'

Janine di Giovanni was an intrepid reporter in Sarajevo, and amongst many of her eye-witness reports of determined attempts at survival in the besieged city there are three that are particularly memorable and disturbing.

Winter is always bitterly cold in the city and that of 1993 was no exception. Janine could smell sewage and open wood fires and there was little food; brandy and French perfume were being sold on the black market at hugely inflated prices and there were rumours that at least 70 per cent of the humanitarian aid was not getting through, a fact hotly denied by the UN.

Janine went to Bjelave where Klea was living in a converted garage with her husband and baby as she had been burnt out of her flat. She had a wood stove which she tried to keep going and had somehow created a tiny kitchen. Klea had lost a great deal of weight but was determined to survive. Sometimes the shelling was so bad that it was impossible to hear anyone talk.

Shortly before Christmas her baby had a cold and Klea had stopped leaving the garage to collect water because she was too frightened of the shells. *'But she is singing that morning,'* Janine di Giovanni writes, *'because she has saved enough flour to make pitta bread to eat with cheese, given to her by a Muslim neighbour. She has saved two potatoes for twenty days to stuff the pitta with, and she is going to make buhtl, a kind of doughnut.'*

Klea considered herself very lucky to find her primitive accommodation, despite the fact that it was only a little way from the front line. She told Janine, *'It's strange how dead my things look now... the television set, the radio. What I miss now are my records. Things like Dire Straits or Bruce Hornsby, or even watching the European Cup. When I finally got evacuated from Dobrinja, I don't know, I must have been crazy, but the first thing I did was ask someone who won the European soccer championship...'*

Fatima was another survivor of Sarajevo who spoke to Janine. She, however, wanted to get back inside the city rather than escape from it - a unique situation to be in. She was 44, had ten children, and was an aid worker.

When the war began, she had been in Vienna working for CARE, preparing to bring supplies of medicine into Sarajevo. Her entire family were in the city and she was unable to get a flight back inside. Fatima was forced to return to the hotel in Vienna and communicate with them by telephone. Eventually the lines were cut and she was left in despair. She could now only reach her husband and children via journalists, who took messages and letters, and through amateur radio enthusiasts. Nevertheless, Fatima was a resourceful woman and she was determined that somehow she was going to reach her beloved family.

Working in Zagreb in Croatia with refugees, she managed to evacuate three of her teenage daughters on one of the final convoys that came out of the besieged city. Then she took the bus to Split, hitchhiked through southern Bosnia and eventually arrived at the checkpoint nearest to Sarajevo. Because she was unable to get any help from the UN, Fatima walked across two highly dangerous front lines with constant shooting. She had a Bosnian soldier as guide and eventually arrived in the suburb of Dobrinja.

Walking towards the centre of the city, she was horrified to find that two thousand graves for soldiers and civilians had been dug in the park where she had often taken her own children to play.

Finally Fatima arrived at her home in Gorica where, thankfully, her family were still living. She found them much changed and she told Janine, *'It made me so sad when the children were telling me the difference between the sound of guns and artillery, the difference between the*

*sound of the general alert and the air strike
alarm. But I was proud of them. No matter how
sorry I felt. I was proud that they had survived in
the worst of conditions.'*

The most tragic example of survival Janine de
Giovanni recounts is that of Nusret Krasnic, who
was nine when she first met him. Although his
parents were killed and Nusret lived in the filthy
squalor of the Ljubica Ivezic orphanage, he managed to escape from the place at least once a
week and, heartbreakingly, on each occasion
tried to get home.

The orphanage was a hell hole, stinking of
boiled food and damp, overrun by rats and with
rain pouring into the windows from which the
glass had been blown out. There were no toilets,
the children hardly washed and they slept nine
to a room, huddled in beds or sleeping bags, with
inadequate clothing and an animalistic existence.
Some were mentally retarded; others were driven
insane.

Janine remembers that Nusret was more like
an animal than a child. She saw a small boy,
hardly three feet (one metre) tall, his skin mot-
tled by the cold, his teeth as sharp as a wild animal's. He came running through the snow
towards her, in boots that were far too big,
accompanied by a dog called Juju who also lived
in the orphanage. Nusret slept with Juju for

warmth and comfort. The boy ran with a decided limp but seemed fearless, hanging on to the back of humanitarian aid trucks for a ride. Since he had arrived in the orphanage, Nusret had hardly spoken, traumatized by his mother having been killed by a shell in front of him. When he occasionally did burst into speech, he only talked of the food his mother had cooked for him. Nusret couldn't write his own name. He had forgotten how to. He had also forgotten any form of civilization. He would only survive if he was sufficiently street-wise and, like Juju, lived the life of an animal.

CHAPTER 6

KIDNAP

Wealthy Italian families are often the victims of highly sophisticated kidnap gangs, who are not only prepared to spin out negotiations for many months but also to use as much duplicity as possible. Often a ransom is paid, but the victim is not released and another ransom is demanded.

So concerned had the Carabinieri (Italian police) become over the kidnap 'business', that in association with the government they had decided to freeze family bank assets so that negotiations could be terminated. So desperate are the families, however, for the safe return of those they have lost that they are prepared to move quickly, transfer assets, change telephone numbers and contact points – anything to prevent the police endangering the life of one of their loved ones.

In the early 1980s, the Brunelli family were well known in the hotel and restaurant business in Rome. They owned the magnificent El Dorado Hotel and a lavish holiday complex known as the Centro Brunelli by the sea half an hour from Rome itself.

On the evening of 10 April 1981, 22-year-old Giuseppe Brunelli was attacked by five men as he rang the bell on the automatic gate of the family home. Had it not been for the rapid action of his father, Renato Brunelli, who grabbed a gun and ran outside firing, his son would have been a kidnap victim. Three months later Nicola, the Brunellis' 13-year-old daughter, was kidnapped near the Brunelli seaside complex. The family had just left the restaurant to walk to their chalet when they discovered they had left the key in reception. Nicola ran back to get it, straight into the arms of the kidnappers.

The Brunelli family had not employed bodyguards, despite the fact that the attack on Giuseppe made it all too clear they had become kidnap targets. Nicola was not allowed to go out unless accompanied by a member of the family, but this was a fatally inadequate precaution.

Six days passed without any word from Nicola's kidnappers, and on the advice of a friend the Brunelli family employed a British security adviser called John Seton, who had worked with Mark Bles, an ex-SAS member and security adviser to wealthy Italian families.

Seton had worked on at least eight cases of kidnap in Rome already and had considerable experience in the complexities of such negotiations. He briefed the family on how to organize a Crisis Management Committee (CMC) and the need to prepare to 'invest' money when deciding on a negotiating budget for the final ransom amount. Seton's tactics were ingenious and could force the kidnappers to end their silence – designed to break down the victim's family –

much sooner than they wanted to. He advised the Brunellis to place a prominent advertisement in a newspaper which would appear to be some kind of coded message. Seton hoped that the real kidnappers would assume that the family were in negotiation with hoaxers. The real gang would be worried that the Brunellis might be just about to hand over the ransom to the hoaxers – money that the actual gang saw as 'rightfully' theirs.

Seton recommended the following message which was duly placed in *Il Messaggero*, on 29 July 1981. It read: *Sea bass on the menu today at our previous price.*

Before the advert appeared, however, two letters arrived from Nicola, one to her parents and a second to her uncle.

Dear Parents,
It is not easy to start a dialogue in circumstances of this sort... When I think that it is because of me that you are suffering, especially Papa who is very ill, I feel I am dying. I don't think it's a good idea to describe the conditions I am being kept in ... I just tell you to offer what is necessary for my release, in particular I beg you to get hold of cash quickly before the magistrate freezes your assets, otherwise I believe my captors will keep me for a long, long time. They are not treating me badly but time

doesn't pass without me thinking of all the difficulties of this restriction. I have been told that for my freedom we need 7,000,000,000 lire. I hope you can do it quickly although I know of the difficulties.

When you are sure of the payment put an advertisement in Il Messaggero, in the Cronica di Roma section, with the following message:

LOST CANARY IN TORVAJANICA. GREEN EYES. BIG REWARD.

The kidnappers will identify themselves through the words

THE SEA IS WARM TO BATHE IN.

I love you very much and please excuse me. Goodbye.
Nicola Brunelli

The second letter, to her uncle, read:

Dear Uncle Stefano,
I am Nicola. I am writing this letter to reassure you about my health and state of mind.
I have already written a letter to my father about contact with the kidnappers and I believe he has received it. The days are passing slowly for me but in spite of everything they are treat-

*ing me quite well. I greet you with all my heart
and please try to keep my Papa calm.*
Nicola Brunelli

(They will identify themselves with the phrase,

THE SEA IS WARM TO BATHE IN.)

A third letter from Nicola arrived the next day,
23 July, addressed to another uncle:

Dear Uncle Marcello,
*I am Nicola, and at this moment I am in the
hands of kidnappers who are not treating me
badly. However I must say they are looking
after my health. They have allowed me to write
a letter to Mama and Papa in which they indicated their instructions for my release and how
contact is to be made. Here every moment of
the day passes slowly and with all sincerity I
cannot see when I will return home. Please do
all you can to keep my parents' morale up and
tell them, please, to pardon me for my mistake
if they can. Many, many greetings.*
Nicola Brunelli

(They will identify themselves with the phrase,

THE SEA IS WARM TO BATHE IN.)

As a result of these letters, Seton concluded

they were dealing with a highly professional and competent gang who were experienced in the kidnap business. There were also similarities with the kidnapping of Giovanni Palombini, an 82-year-old industrialist who had been taken on 17 April 1981. He had not been seen since.

Seton believed that the Brunellis must budget for a final payment of between 700 and 800 million lire. A first payment could be in the region of 275 million lire. The adverts began to be placed and at 9.02 p.m. on 30 July, the family was contacted and their offer of 280 million lire turned down – at least for the moment.

'We are not a Sardinian gang, or a bunch of chicken thieves, or rabbits,' explained the kidnapper. *'When you are ready with a conspicuous amount, place the advertisement.'*

Seton had reckoned that as the gang's spokesman had made no specific demand the price must therefore be negotiable, and the family could then put up a reasonable second offer. For the moment, Seton was keeping up a damage limitation exercise. He also thought that the gang were deliberately giving the family the impression they wanted to reach a fast, painless settlement so that a first payment would be made. Then they would be ready to demand a second.

Whilst these subtle negotiations were taking place, however, Nicola was determined to survive her ordeal. When she was first attacked she put up a spirited defence, just as her brother Giuseppe had done. The kidnappers were waiting for her in an Alfa Romeo and she was just closing the door of the chalet when someone shouted, 'She's the one!'

Nicola turned to face them and they grabbed her by her arms and legs. Being tall and strong – she looked older than her thirteen years – she almost managed to escape, knocking one man down by kicking him. The other three, however, carried her bodily to the car and Nicola went into shock.

The kidnappers drove off but quickly changed vehicles. They put sticky tape over Nicola's eyes and ears and clapped on handcuffs that tightened the harder she struggled. They drove for approximately twenty minutes to a house in the country and she spent the first night in the back of the car. Nicola told her kidnappers several times that her father was ill, but they only told her not to worry as everything would soon be over.

The next morning she was blindfolded and taken to a house, where she was kept for only a day. She knew the Polizia were active because she could hear the sirens, and she prayed they would somehow manage to find her quickly. She was still in a state of shock and understood little of what was going on. Because of this, she remained relatively calm, stoically hoping to be rescued. But as the gang repeatedly told her the Polizia and the Carabinieri were useless she soon began to lose hope for 'official' rescue. Nicola knew, however, that her family were powerful and would use every possible means to come to her aid.

Over the next three months she was moved five times. At first she was kept in a tent which was inside a room and near a kitchen, although she rarely received any hot food. Her kidnappers gave her tinned tomatoes or ham, and the diet was occasionally varied with pizza, biscuits, pastry, chocolate, or scrambled and boiled eggs. She grew thoroughly weary of tinned tuna fish and Philadelphia cream cheese which were constantly on the menu. Fortunately, she didn't have much appetite. Nicola only spoke to one or two of the gang, although she later realized they were at least thirty to thirty-five strong.

For the first three days, the kidnappers had brutally kept the sticky tape over Nicola's eyes, and when they took it off it was some time before she could see again. She was given a portable toilet which was only emptied every few days. Her wrists were still badly bruised by the handcuffs and there was no bed, only a mattress. Nicola's hands and feet were chained to two heavy lumps of concrete.

In the first month she hoped every day to be freed. The gang told her, *'We have called your family and tomorrow you'll be going home.'* The continuous repetition of this statement nearly broke her.

Seton meanwhile had drawn up a strategy plan in order to dupe the gang into believing the Brunellis had less money than they had originally thought. It was highly ingenious and read as follows:

1. The family should attempt to sell one of their four restaurants to raise cash for the ransom. If their employees demonstrated against the sale, however, they could prevent it. Press reports would show the family doing its best to raise money but running into prolonged labour disputes.

2. A member of the family could be arrested for illegally importing money which would receive widespread publicity. Understandably, however, the Brunellis were uncomfortable with this suggestion as it would undermine their reputation for all time. Alternatively, a family member might be arrested leaving a bank or a friend's

house with a large quantity of money. This could be staged with the Carabinieri's co-operation and would be seen by the press as a new drive by the judiciary to prevent ransom payments. It could also mean the family would be able to claim that the confiscated money was no longer available to be used as part of the ransom. As a result, the gang might be persuaded to settle for what they could get. (Seton had successfully used this ruse before in other negotiations.)

3. A 'robbery' involving a large sum of money could be reported from one of the brothers' houses or the hotel.

Eventually the gang contacted the family, and their offer was increased to 450 million lire. The kidnappers, however, completely unrattled, informed the family they were a long way away from what was required and told Marcello Brunelli to get a bank loan. He was also warned that Nicola's ordeal might continue for some considerable time if there was no financial resolution. The Brunellis were advised to place the now familiar advertisement in the paper when they had decided to make their daughter's abductors a better offer.

John Seton, however, took all this in his stride, reckoning that the reference to the bank loan meant that the gang realized there were limits to the amount of cash the family could actually raise themselves.

On Saturday 22 August, and day thirty-seven of the kidnap, the gang rang to express disappointment with the negotiations and to say that there would be no more contact for a month – a deadly weapon when the family were suffering to such a desperate extent.

Meanwhile the police, low-key since the first days of the abduction, began to put pressure on, telling Brunelli that they would block the line after each call from the kidnappers' representative in an attempt to trace him. They had recently had some success in another kidnap case in which they had used the same tactics, and were riding high. But despondency spread when the Canary advertisements were spotted by the press and speculative features were run on Nicola's abduction, noting the similarity with the actions of the Palombini kidnap gang.

The negotiations continued, with offers being made and rejected, and a great deal of psychological pressure being applied by the kidnappers. Renato Brunelli was becoming ill with worry and broke down several times during the repeated telephone calls, so it was decided that all future calls would be taken by his wife, Maria. At last the moment for dropping the ransom money seemed to be coming closer, but the issue was then further complicated by the action of one of the Italian judges, who wrote to all banks asking them to report back when the Brunelli ransom money was withdrawn. Judge Cordova then went further by applying a new law which laid down that anyone depositing or withdrawing 50,000 or 100,000 lire notes had to provide identification and a legitimate address. She was determined to try and catch kidnappers who were laundering their ransom monies through the banks.

Despite this unwelcome intervention the drop of 800 million lire was carried out on 20 September, sixty days after Nicola had been taken, but despite Seton's conviction that it would be a one-off and Nicola would be released, this was not to be. The next evening the gang's negotiator, 'Alphonso', said the ransom had been paid in dirty money and he would therefore expect another 800 million lire.

Seton was understandably mortified that his intuition had been so gravely at fault, but he still felt the gang could be made to feel vulnerable if only he could persuade them that they were endangering the highly lucrative Rome kidnap business by demanding double payments. Seton's theory was that if ransom payments failed to produce the return of the victim, families would simply stop paying ransoms. He was also certain that Alphonso was sufficiently intelligent to understand the risks he was running.

Seton also wondered if the gang was part of a larger organization which might pressure this current 'cell' into settling for what they had already received. Also, if the gang could now be convinced that the Brunellis had lost any hope of seeing Nicola alive again, it would undermine their position. The family's most powerful ally now would be the press, and Seton began to devise stories that could be run. The Brunellis naturally had friends in the press who could help to place the articles.

Now the second financial demand had been made by the kidnappers, the family were indeed almost at breaking point, particularly when another letter arrived from Nicola. It read:

'It has come to my knowledge that you haven't received my previous letter. It must be because there was a strike on the railways and other things. I have been assured that the present letter will be delivered directly so I renew hope that you will conclude as soon as possible this

endless imprisonment. Don't trust the forces of the state, i.e. for the reward and the other stupid things. The truth is: words don't resolve anything unfortunately. If you do not again give the payment requested it will be difficult to see me again. My custodians are severe but I believe in their word. They are not like the others. I can't foresee the hour when I will come to embrace you. I really miss you. A very dear greeting to you all from your dear Nicola.

It was accompanied by a missive from the gang:

Respected Brunelli
As your daughter has clearly illustrated, the fact that the letter has not been delivered previously is not our fault.
We repeat that the sea is warm to bathe in. It is substituted with

A HARE RUNS FASTER THAN A DOG

The advertisement in Il Messaggero *– Female Canary etc. etc. has to be changed to the phrase: "Lost dog – Poodle, White, Villa Pamphili. Big Reward."*
When you are sure that you can obtain our request, ONLY THEN, place your advertisement. We want 900 million, we don't give any impor-

tance to the blocking [of assets], *or your health, or other things. If you want, it won't be difficult to conclude. To be fair to you I understand that the previous people didn't keep their word. We can't judge them. We guarantee our words with the highest honesty.*

Rosario.

It was now clear to Seton that the gang were trying to prove they were not the same kidnappers as the ones who had taken Palombini, and who had successfully negotiated two large ransoms without returning him.

Negotiations dragged on but, ironically, in the end it was the police who eventually saved Nicola. A wanted criminal and suspected kidnapper was run to earth in a shoot-out at a villa in Lavinio, a seaside resort near Torvajanica. The police eventually broke in to find a man named De Sanctis holding Nicola as a shield and brandishing a pistol. But he was already wounded and rapidly overpowered. Nicola, weak and unable to walk, was saved on the hundredth day of her kidnap. She was filthy, with very long fingernails, and as one reporter wrote, *'her hair stuck together as if it was smeared with glue.'*

Nevertheless, she was free at last, although Palombini was eventually discovered dead.

Nicola later stated: *'Looking back on it all, I thought they wanted to kill me. I was sure of that. It didn't seem possible to me that my family could pay the money.'*

Her memories of the ordeal were confused, as she had lost all sense of time. Every night when she went to sleep, Nicola heard music downstairs and sometimes there was the sound of people playing tennis. She knew she was not far from Torvajanica because of the short distance they had travelled in the car, but the kidnappers wanted to make her believe they were from Milan and they even went to the extent of assuming Milanese accents.

The gang gave Nicola newspapers, puzzles, games books and she drew a lot, although they regularly checked what she was drawing. She had to write the four letters which they dictated to her. *'I didn't want to write them but they told me to and they told me to say I was ill when I wasn't. I was just tired and sad. They threatened me with a pistol to make me do it.'*

Clearly the gang had learned to respect Nicola's strong spirit. They told her that they had imagined a girl would cry and were surprised at her stoicism. They had not reckoned on the strength of her personality and found they were being given an object lesson in the powers of female endurance. However, without the police's lucky break, it is more than likely that Nicola Brunelli would had suffered the same fate as Giovanni Palombini.

CHAPTER 7

THE SLAVE WHO ESCAPED

"Canada was often spoken of as the only sure refuge from pursuit and that blessed land was now the desire of my longing heart."

Josiah Henson, a slave on a plantation in the deep South of America, wrote these words. He was born on 15 June 1789, in Charles County, Maryland, about a mile from Port Tobacco. After years of suffering at the hands of a succession of brutal slave masters, Josiah made up his mind to escape to Canada where slavery was illegal. Josiah had a large family and knew they would have to make the most appalling journey. His wife, however, only agreed to join Josiah when he told her that he was prepared to go without her, taking the older children with him.

'With tears and supplications she besought me to remain at home, contented. In vain I explained to her our liability to be torn asunder at any moment; the horrors of the slavery I had lately seen; the happiness we should enjoy together in a land of freedom, safe from all pursuing harm.'

Armed with a knapsack of tough cloth in which Josiah planned to carry the two youngest children, the family set out. It was the middle of September and a dark, moonless night when they embarked on the river in a small skiff that a fellow slave had loaned him.

'It was an anxious moment. We sat still as death. In the middle of the stream the good fellow said to me, "It will be the end of me if this is ever found out, but you won't be brought back alive, Sie, will you?"'

Josiah was determined that he wouldn't, and once over the river he and his family walked on the roads by night and hid during the day, deep in the woods. By this stage their scanty provisions were giving out, and they were exhausted and hungry. The children cried all night from hunger, and Josiah's wife reproached him bitterly.

'It was a bitter thing to hear them cry, and God knows I needed encouragement myself. My limbs were weary, and my back and shoulders raw with the burden I carried. A fearful dread of detection ever pursued me, and I would start out of my sleep in terror, my heart beating against my ribs, expecting to find the dogs and slave-hunters after me. Had I been alone I would have borne starvation, even to exhaustion, before I would have ventured in sight of a house in quest of food.'

Despite his fear, Josiah knew he had to feed his family somehow, and he set out towards the south again to put people off his scent. He knew he would have to beg and also knew that his reception would be hostile.

Predictably, the first householder told Josiah he had no food for blacks and so did the second. His wife, however, was more compassionate and told her husband, *'How can you treat any human being so? If a dog was hungry, I would give him something to eat.'* Then she added, *'We have children, and who knows but they may some day need the help of a friend.'* She asked Josiah into the house and loaded a plate with venison and bread. When he tried to pay her, she returned his money and gave them more food. *'I felt the hot tears roll down my cheeks as she said, "God bless you", and I hurried away to bless my starving* wife and little ones.'

The venison was very salty and the next problem was the growing thirst of the children. Disregarding danger yet again, Josiah stole out one more, praying he wouldn't excite suspicion. Could his luck last, or was he risking so much that he would soon be captured?

'I went off stealthily, breaking the bushes to keep my path, to find water. I found a little rill, and drank a large draught. Then I tried to carry some in my hat; but, alas! it leaked. Finally, I took off both shoes, which luckily had no holes in them, rinsed them out, filled them with water, and carried it to my family. They drank it with great delight. I have since then sat at splendidly furnished tables in Canada, the United States, and England; but never did I see any human beings relish anything more than my poor famishing little ones did that refreshing draught out of their father's shoes.'

The family continued the journey, travelling by night and resting by day, until they arrived at Scioto where they had been told they should follow the military road that had been constructed in the last war with Great Britain.

Eventually, Josiah found the road, flanked at its beginning with large sycamore and elm trees, but what they hadn't been told was that it ran through a dangerous wilderness. There were no houses to beg from and Josiah had few rations left. In fact, all he had was a small piece of dried beef. The family shared the meagre food by their camp fire that night – to the accompaniment of the howling of hungry wolves.

Next morning they started out again, and Josiah wrote: 'A painful day it was to us. The road was rough, the underbrush tore our clothes and exhausted our strength; trees that had been blown down blocked the way; we were faint with hunger; and no prospect of relief opened up before us. We spoke little, but steadily struggled along; I with my babes on my back, my wife aiding the two other children to climb over the fallen trunks and force themselves through the briers. Suddenly, as I was plodding along a little ahead of my wife and the boys, I heard them call me, and turning round saw my wife prostrate on the ground. "Mother's dying," cried Tom.'

At first, Josiah thought his wife was dead, and for some minutes there seemed no life in her at all. Then she opened her eyes, took a few mouthfuls of beef broth and gradually a little strength returned. She was suffering from severe exhaustion and had fallen trying to get over a large log.

'... we once more went bravely on our way. I cheered the sad group with hopes I was far from sharing myself. For the first time I was nearly ready to abandon myself to despair. Starvation in

the wilderness was the doom that stared me and mine in the face.'

Later that afternoon, the family met up with a group of Indians who were terrified of their black skin. They ran away, but Josiah bravely followed until he arrived at their wigwams. Eventually he met the chief who told his so-called braves that black people wouldn't harm them. Now curiosity replaced their original alarm.

'Each one wanted to touch the children, who were as shy as partridges with their long life in the woods; and as they shrunk away, and uttered a little cry of alarm, the Indian would jump back too, as if he thought they would bite him. However, a little while sufficed to make them understand what we were, and whither we were going, and what we needed; and as little to set them about supplying our wants, feeding us bountifully, and giving us a comfortable wigwam for our night's rest.'

That evening Josiah and his family discovered that they were nearing the Canadian border. Next morning they thanked the Indians and hurried on, a new hope beginning to build up inside them.

In the huge plain of Ohio they arrived at a stream that crossed the road. Josiah experimentally forded the water with the help of a sounding pole, and then took his children over on his back, returning to fetch his wife. Resting afterwards, Josiah discovered that a large patch of skin on his back was worn away, where his knapsack had rubbed his bare skin.

West of Sandusky City, he hid his family and walked on towards one of the great lakes that border North America and Canada, approaching some men loading a small coaster. He asked for work and was immediately employed, without any questions being asked.

Later, however, Josiah admitted his plight to the captain, who agreed to take him and his family to Buffalo, which was just across the river from Canada. The captain told Josiah that he would lay his ship just opposite a nearby island in the lake and send a boat across to pick up his new passengers. He added that he was taking this precaution because there were gangs of slave catchers in the town whose suspicions would be alerted immediately if Josiah brought his family out of the bush during the day.

As he helped to load the hatches with bushels of corn, Josiah wondered if he could really trust this benign captain. He seemed too generous, too good to be true. Was he not just setting a trap? But Josiah would rather have died than return to slavery on the plantations, and he knew he had no option than to trust his new benefactor.

'I watched the vessel with intense interest as she

left her moorings. *Away she went before the free breeze. Already she seemed beyond the spot at which the captain agreed to lay to, and still she flew along. My heart sunk within me; so near deliverance, and again to have my hopes blasted, again to be cast on my own resources. I felt that they had been making a mock of my misery. The sun had sunk to rest, and the purple and gold of the west were fading away into grey. Suddenly, however, as I gazed with weary heart, the vessel swung round into the wind, the sails flapped, and she stood motionless. A moment more, and a boat was lowered from her stern, and with steady stroke made for the point at which I stood. I felt that my hour of release had come. On she came, and in ten minutes she rode up handsomely on to the beach.'*

Aided by his new friends from the ship, Josiah searched for his family in the undergrowth but, to his horror, he could only find one of the children. Realizing that the captain wouldn't wait much longer, Josiah had now almost given up hope of getting his family across to Canada.

Then, to his enormous relief, he found his wife and discovered that she had been deeply alarmed at his long absence. Imagining he had fallen into the hands of one of the gangs who were trying to return escaping slaves to their masters – at a price – she had gone into terrified hiding.

But now, at last, Josiah and his family were safely together, and as they embarked their luggage on the boat the captain had sent to pick them up he knew they would soon be in Canada, and would never have to suffer the painful indignity of being slaves again. And in his desperate struggle for survival, Josiah had also discovered something else — the unexpected kindness of some of the individuals he had come across. The woman who had given him and his family meat, the friendly Indians and the captain and crew who had not let him down. After years of slavery and of being beaten and humiliated, Josiah was deeply moved.

CHAPTER 8

THE BURNING OF
SIMON WESTON

It was 1982 and the Falklands War was well under way. A soldier was shouting down the length of the tank deck, 'Air-raid warning Red! Air-raid warning Red! Get down! Get down!'

Simon Weston was facing the stern of the *Sir Galahad* at the time and he crouched down, looking up at the open deck above him, trying to catch a glimpse of the enemy Argentine plane. The ship was known as an LSL, landing ship logistic, and Weston had been aboard her before, as a Welsh Guardsman en route to Northern Ireland. She weighed 5765 tons (5674 tonnes) and carried 68 crew of the Royal Fleet Auxiliary. The *Sir Galahad* could reach a speed of 17 knots, carried two 40 mm guns, had a helicopter deck and over a long period could carry 340 troops or 534 over a short time. Like a car ferry, she had a high stern with a ramp, a flat bottom that caused her to roll horribly and bow doors that opened sideways. She was highly vulnerable to bombing attacks as she approached Bluff Cove in the Falklands.

Whilst the *Sir Galahad* was heading towards her destination, it was belatedly discovered that the direct channel to Bluff Cove was too shallow for her and she was forced to head up to Fitzroy and drop anchor in the bay, near her sister ship, the *Sir Tristram*.

When Major Ewen Southby-Tailyour, a Royal

Marine officer, arrived he was horrified by the sight of the *Sir Galahad* anchored in broad daylight in such an exposed position and full of troops. He came across on one of her landing craft and suggested that the troops were moved to the safety of the shore, but this suggestion was turned down on the grounds that the landing craft was still full of ammunition and it was a regulation that soldiers should not travel with explosives. A long argument followed, but it was eventually decided that the regulation could not be broken. The Welsh Guards remained on board, an easy target for the Argentine air force.

The bomb came through the port side of the ship and across Simon Weston's position, and for a split second he saw the plane, a grey streak flying from right to left. Jet engines screamed from the planes above and there was a brilliant flash from the engine room, yellow and orange in colour, rather like an oil rig flare. Weston wrote: '*A moment later there was the warmth of summer in the air, only there was no breeze, nothing moving at all. Nobody did anything. Nobody said anything.*'

Then a cloud moved towards the soldiers and they quietly watched it engulf them. The man next to Weston was standing very still. Suddenly everyone sprang back to life as if a film had been stopped and started again. But the film was a negative. Men were shadows, silhouettes with *'brilliant, whole-body haloes of the most beautiful colours I have ever seen – a sunburst that I could touch and yet couldn't touch: it was touching me, I couldn't touch back.'*

Weston was aware that the breath had been sucked from his lungs and then there was a surge of hot air. But he couldn't feel anything. He was later told that in the first flash of the bomb all his exposed nerve ends had been scorched away.

Weston gazed down at the backs of his hands, and to his horror saw that they looked as if they were frying and then melting, *'the skin bubbling and flaking away from the bone like the leaves of a paperback burning on a bonfire before being carried away by the wind.'*

Looking around him unbelievingly, Weston saw that his friends were in an appalling state. A man he recognized was lying on the floor and he tried to lift him, but his uniform was blazing and the flames burnt away Weston's palms.

His hands then felt strangely slippery, *'as if they had wet soap on them and I was trying to grasp an aluminium pole.'* Weston let the man go and then saw to his horror that many layers of his own skin were embedded in the dying man's combat jacket. His hands were completely raw but, for the moment, there was still no pain.

Simon Weston had been a macho youngster, always looking for excitement and getting into trouble at home in Wales until he had a brush with the police. He was ebullient, determined, and sufficiently stoic and afraid of boredom at home to become a Guardsman. He was friendly, a good mixer, and as a result his reaction to this catastrophe was not only a natural instinct for survival himself but also a desire to help his mates.

His recall of the appalling incident is total; as he gazed round at the bodies that were either burning or smouldering on the floor, the vivid colours that the bomb had created were permanently etched into his mind.

'It was like watching the Northern Lights, but from only a few feet away, and against a sky that was profoundly, impenetrably black. A kaleidoscope of colours – reds, browns, yellows, golds unbelievably intense, more beautiful than anything I had ever seen, dancing around my friends and then enveloping them in flames. Two lads in front of me danced reels in the rainbow, jerking and writhing to a silent tune of death, and there was nothing I could do.'

It was the silence that made Weston so detached, the silence and the lack of pain.

But the silence was not to last for long. Suddenly the sound came back, and with it the awesome reality of men trying to beat the flames from their bodies, running around in circles and screaming like animals. He could hear the voices of men he knew, friends who were dying, and Weston stood transfixed as black and choking smoke began to fill the space around him.

He could smell the stench of burning metal and roasting human flesh, and his instinct for self-preservation finally conquered his instinct to help his mates. There was nothing wrong with that – there was nothing he could do for any of them – but he didn't know which way to go.

It would have seemed impossible for the situation to have got any worse. But it did.

This part of the *Sir Galâhad* also contained a large consignment of petrol for the Land Rovers and it was now flowing from jerry cans, igniting in vast sheets of flame as it came out. Vaporized diesel blew back from the engine room, a fireball erupted and the 81 mm mortar bombs began to heat up. Because of the increase in temperature, grenades and bullets began to explode. Metal whizzed past Weston's head as he groped about in the dark while the black smoke increased, a dark blanket that would suffocate him unless he was burnt alive by the flames or blown to fragments by shrapnel.

In despair, Weston tried to find his gun so he could put himself out of this searing misery, and as he searched for it he heard men begging him to put them out of their pain, to end the hell of it all now.

Then, miraculously, Weston felt a ripple in the smoke on his face and knew that this meant fresh air was flowing from somewhere. This hint of escape, however, seemed to be in the worst possible position as the air was flowing through a wall of flame. As he heard the sound of ammunition going off behind him, Weston's instincts took over again and he charged at the barrier.

As he ran through the flames, Weston had one final image from hell, one that, above all others, would remain in his mind for the rest of his life. Blown against the bulkhead by the force of the explosion, a man looked as if he was being crucified. Something unidentifiable was keeping him upright, but whatever it was he was desperately trying to release himself with his bayonet, stabbing at his back, trying to cut himself free of his clothing or prise himself off the bulkhead or both. Weston shouted to him but he didn't reply so he ran on through the flames.

Weston ran on towards the exit, eventually arriving in a corridor to find soldiers collapsed from shock but not burnt. He came to a door but was unable to open it with his raw hands. A CSM (Company Sergeant Major) swung it open for him and a marine told him to keep running up a flight of stairs. He was told he would be safe at the top.

Weston remembers that the marine gazed at him in horror. He felt the glorious draught well before he saw the final exit. The air was cool and clean and sweet as Weston charged up the stairs.

The huge pall of black smoke hung over the *Sir Galahad* in the still air of a beautiful afternoon. Men lay around the deck, charred and blackened, with much of their skin burnt away, and Weston sucked air into his lungs, now in considerable shock himself. There was little panic and a guardsman told him to lie down on the deck while he fetched a medical officer.

Together, he and the medic cut away Simon Weston's clothes and took the syringe of morphine from the lapel of his jacket (all troops carried these) and injected the drug into his arm.

All Weston was obsessed about was whether his private parts were untouched and in working order. The medic assured him that they were.

Sea King and Wessex helicopters had already converged on the *Sir Galahad*, and Weston watched them fly through the dense smoke trying to get men off the ship and out of the sea. One of the Sea Kings eventually winched him up, and from his vantage point he could see that the *Sir Tristram* had also been hit. He later discovered that there were 143 casualties, 46 of whom were dead.

Simon Weston was eventually flown back to England where he underwent thirty-nine operations to his face, hands and legs. He had 46 per cent burns.

The *Sir Galahad*, which was still burning two weeks after the bombing, was towed some twenty kilometres into the South Atlantic and sunk. She is now an official war grave for those who didn't survive.

After his many operations Simon Weston continued mentally as well as physically to fight for his recovery, involving himself in a number of challenging activities. They included a goodwill tour of Australia, Operation Raleigh projects such as cutting a track around the Kelper Mountains in New Zealand, founding a youth training organization called Weston Spirit and learning to fly.

CHAPTER 9

MOON LANDING

Although Michael Collins was not to step on to the moon's surface himself, he had to take enormous personal responsibility for the lives of Neil Armstrong and Buzz (Edwin) Aldrin, the astronauts who did.

After years of training and medical checks, the three-man crew of *Apollo 11* were ready to make that incredible leap for mankind, to leave our planet for the moon and begin the exploration of space.

The voyage, in July 1969, was to take eight days and, in Collins' view, presented eleven major problems for the crew.

1 THE LAUNCH

The most hazardous time of all, with the huge engines throwing out high-temperature exhaust gases with enormous wind blasts as the rocket ascended.

2 TLI

Trans-lunar injection. This meant firing the Saturn V engine for the final time, putting *Apollo 11* on course for the moon.

3 T AND D

Transportation and docking were Michael Collins's personal responsibility. He was to fly the command module out in front of the Saturn V (the rocket), turn round and then dock with the lunar module nestling up the Saturn's nose. He was then to pull the lunar module free.

4 LOI

Lunar orbit insertion. This was the process of slowing down sufficiently to be captured by the gravity of the moon, but not going so slowly that they would hit the surface.

5 LMD

Lunar module descent. An exacting time for Neil Armstrong and Buzz Aldrin – who were to enter the lunar module, leaving Collins in the command module, in orbit – because they had to come down at exactly the right location on the moon.

6 LANDING ON THE MOON

This was the untested part of the operation, and was the subject of much apprehension and conjecture. Two hypothetical problems were much discussed. Firstly, because the fuel tanks would be empty, the craft could sink into the thick dust that many scientists thought they might find on the moon's surface. Secondly, static electricity might cause the dust to stick to the windscreen, obscuring visibility

7 EVA

Walking on the moon, technically known as extra-vehicular activity, could be exhausting and there was always the possibility of injury or damage to the equipment. There could even be surface weakness which meant the ground could collapse beneath their feet.

8 LIFT-OFF FROM THE MOON

Unless the engines in the module worked, Neil Armstrong and Buzz Aldrin would be stranded on the moon's surface for ever.

9 RENDEZVOUS

This was the most complicated part of the whole procedure, and it had been established there could be eighteen different types of rendezvous as a result of the situation going wrong. A large number of these options involved Collins rescuing Armstrong and Aldrin in a variety of different ways.

10 TEI

Trans-earth injection, which meant igniting the command module's engine so that it was able to gain sufficient speed to break the gravity pull of the moon and send *Apollo 11* back to earth.

11 ENTRY

It was essential to dive back into the earth's atmosphere at exactly the right angle. If this angle was too shallow, for instance, *Apollo 11* might miss the earth completely. If the angle was too steep, the spacecraft might burn up.

The crew's only hope lay in the fact that many of these procedures had been successfully rehearsed by earlier flights. Schirra's crew on *Apollo 7* (October 1968) had checked the command module, and Borman on *Apollo 8* (December 1968) had actually taken the module all the way to the moon. McDivitt on *Apollo 9* had test-flown the lunar module while Stafford on *Apollo 10* (March 1969) had conducted a complete rehearsal in lunar orbit, including everything but a landing. Nevertheless, all three crew on *Apollo 11* were decidedly uneasy.

As the mission was composed of two spacecraft, it would be too confusing to call them both *Apollo 11* on the radio. Collins therefore gave the name *Eagle* to the lunar module, and *Columbia* to the command module.

At nine seconds before lift-off, the engines of the Saturn (the launch rocket) were ignited, the clamps on the launch pad were released and *Apollo 11* was on the way to the moon.

The first few seconds were both jerky and noisy and the crew were all relieved when they were over, but as *Apollo 11* climbed out over the Atlantic, Michael Collins noticed with considerable satisfaction that all his dials and instruments were working perfectly.

After exactly 90 seconds, the first stage of the rocket shut down and fell into the sea, and the second stage, with its five engines, took over. At nine minutes after take-off this second stage was discarded and *Apollo 11* was left with the single engine of the third stage to send the mission into orbit.

Finally, at eleven minutes and 42 seconds after lift-off, the *Apollo 11*, with its two components, *Eagle* and *Columbia*, was in orbit, a hundred miles up and travelling at a speed of 18,000 miles per hour.

The first dangerous step was over; there were only ten more to go.

When the time came for transportation and docking, the manoeuvre by which *Columbia* would be attached nose-to-nose to *Eagle*, Collins had to fly *Columbia* away from the Saturn and then turn round to come back and dock with *Eagle*.

This was his first chance to fly *Columbia*. After separating and turning around, he approached *Eagle*, now looking like a mechanical spider crouched against the Saturn. Collins brought the two vehicles together gently, with a slight bump as *Columbia*'s docking probe linked with *Eagle*'s drogue. Then he slipped down out of his couch and into *Columbia*'s tunnel, removing the docking probe as he went.

Collins's next job was to connect a couple of wires so that *Eagle* could receive electricity from

Columbia. Then he pressed a switch which separated *Eagle* from the Saturn and allowed the two modules to float free. The Saturn was redundant now – an empty shell which would soon begin to orbit the sun.

With yet another problem behind them and so far an accident-free record, the crew of *Apollo 11* began to crawl out of their pressure suits and stow them away in bags. This made the inside of *Columbia* appear much larger and more hospitable. The crew felt increasingly safe in the command module, providing they did not lose the connection with *Eagle*. If that happened, all the air would be sucked out and they would die.

Collins had already checked the tunnel connections to *Eagle* several times but was now beginning to worry about temperatures inside both modules. As *Apollo 11* was between the earth and the moon and therefore in constant sunlight, positioning was crucial. If the spacecraft remained, the side facing the sun would become far too hot and the side in the shadow would become too cold. If the modules got overheated the propellant tank pressures would rise dangerously high while the radiators would freeze if the modules became too cold. To prevent either of these disastrous situations occurring, the crew had to position *Apollo 11* broadside to the sun and then turn her slowly round.

With plenty of time to get used to the interior of *Columbia*, Collins discovered that weightlessness made the spacecraft seem completely different from how she had been on earth. On earth the tunnel, for example, was an unused area overhead, but once in space it turned into a resting place where a person could sit, out of the way of everyone else. All three astronauts found that it was possible to wedge themselves into corners or tunnels without being belted in.

Day 2 was so quiet that Collins even had time to exercise. He found a spot near the navigator's panel that was just wide enough to allow his body to stretch out, with his arms over his head touching one wall and his feet another. In this position, he could 'run'. With medical sensors still attached to his chest, Collins could discover from Houston the exact rate of his heart beat. He exercised until the rate doubled, from fifty to one hundred beats per minute. On the same day, the astronauts used their TV camera to show the world what their small planet looked like from a distance of 130,000 miles.

As *Apollo* neared its destination, the change in the moon's appearance was spectacular. A huge sphere filled *Columbia*'s largest window, its underside bulging out towards them and its surface receding towards the edges.

The moon was between them and the sun and

Apollo 11 was now in its sinister shadow. The sun created a halo around it, making the moon's surface dark and mysterious in comparison to its shining rim. Even more eerily, the moon's surface was lit by earthshine – the sunshine that bounces off the surface of the earth on to the surface of the moon. This cast a bluish glow, by which the crew of the *Apollo 11* could see large craters and darker, flat areas known as maria, or seas.

To get into orbit around the moon, the spacecraft had to slow down to avoid shooting past her objective. The crew fired *Columbia*'s rocket engine shortly after *Apollo 11* swung round behind the moon's left edge, out of touch with the earth for the first time. Her own computer told the crew which way to point and how long to fire the engine.

After slightly over six minutes of engine firing, the computer told the astronauts they had arrived, and the spacecraft skimmed along about sixty miles above the moon's pockmarked surface. The dark side of the moon has been a source of mystery to scientists for all time and the reality was not disappointing. It looked sombre, disconcerting, its terrain scarred by the impact of meteorites over billions of years.

As there is no atmosphere surrounding the moon to produce clouds or fog, the astronauts' view was impeded only by darkness. Slowly they began to realize that the appearance of the surface changed as the position of the sun altered.

With the sun directly overhead, the moon appeared benign, with soft rounded craters bathed in a rose-coloured light. As the sun shifted toward the lunar horizon, the craters began to cast long shadows, the rose colour changed to dark grey, and the surface became a series of jagged edges. When the sun was below the horizon, the surface was either barely visible if it was in earthshine, or totally invisible if there was no earthshine.

The crew of *Apollo 11* were anxious to find their landing site. The astronauts had been studying maps for months, memorizing a series of craters and other checkpoints leading up to the site. But when the location was made, it looked rough.

Before he went to bed, Collins took several measurements on a crater in an area called the Foaming Sea, east of their landing site in the Sea of Tranquillity. (These seas, of course, are land that gave the impression of water to early astronomers.)

Lunar landing (day 5) began with the normal wake-up call from Houston. After breakfast, the three astronauts returned to their pressure suits. Neil Armstrong and Buzz Aldrin had already put on special underwear, into which thin plastic tubes had been woven. Water would be pumped from their back-packs into their suits and then through the tubes. This would cool their bodies while they were on the hot lunar surface.

Armstrong and Aldrin descended in the *Eagle* which looked like a large gold, black and grey bug hanging in space. Collins's main job was to keep the *Columbia* running and listen to the historic conversation between *Eagle* and Houston.

A temporary blip occurred when Armstrong told Houston his computer was acting strangely, but he was told to continue towards his landing. In fact, the computer-controlled descent was taking *Eagle* down towards an area covered with huge boulders, so Armstrong was forced to find a smoother place, thus using up a lot more fuel than had been calculated.

Once landed, Armstrong and Aldrin decided to abandon their scheduled four-hour sleep and immediately begin to explore the strange, alien world of silence and rock that had no gravity. The surface was level and thankfully firm, and Armstrong, first to set foot on the moon, found he could keep his balance in the strange gravitational field where everything weighed only one sixth of its earth weight.

As they moved amongst the lunar rocks, Neil Armstrong and Buzz Aldrin were contacted by

President Nixon, who told them: *'Neil and Buzz, I am talking to you by telephone from the Oval Office at the White House, and this certainly has to be the most historic telephone call ever made ... Because of what you have done, the heavens have become a part of man's world. As you talk to us from the Sea of Tranquillity, it inspires us to redouble our efforts to bring peace and tranquillity to Earth.'*

Armstrong replied in suitably patriotic terms and planted the United States flag on the surface of the moon.

They then began to gather up some rock samples. To Collins, both astronauts sounded fit and well, but he remained deeply apprehensive, worrying that some lunar-inspired disaster would suddenly occur, something they hadn't calculated, weren't prepared for. He was deeply relieved when they returned safely to *Eagle* and the door was locked.

All three astronauts were now scheduled to sleep for a few hours, so that they would be ready for the demanding rendezvous.

At this stage, Collins was concerned that procedures had gone so well that to have an accident now could be largely his fault. Although he had never been destined to be a man on the moon, there was no doubt he was the man who could kill both Neil Armstrong and Buzz Aldrin.

Collins was nervous – more nervous than at any other time on the flight. If the *Eagle*'s engines failed to work, there was nothing he could do to rescue his companions. He would have to fly home on his own, leaving his close friends to die. They only had enough oxygen to survive for one more day at the most.

Collins could hardly bear the countdown, but thankfully it was successful, pushing *Eagle* into orbit below and behind *Columbia*. He radioed: *'Eagle, Columbia passing over the landing site. It sure is great to look down there and not see you.'*

In fact he hadn't been able to see them on the surface at all, but knowing Armstrong and Aldrin were back in orbit again was an incredible relief.

Finally, the two spacecraft were side-by-side and Collins's computer told him they were in precisely the right position as *Eagle* overtook

Columbia. The docking went according to plan and Buzz Aldrin was first through the hatch. *'I was going to kiss him, but then I got embarrassed and just shook his hand,'* wrote Collins.

For a couple of minutes the three astronauts just floated, admiring the two shiny silver boxes filled with moon rocks. Then it was time to leave *Eagle* in lunar orbit, fire up *Columbia*'s huge engine, and take off for home.

The astronauts paid particular attention to the direction *Columbia* was pointed, for if a mistake was made the spacecraft would hit the moon instead of returning to earth.

After the burn was over, Houston radioed that their radar tracking stations indicated *Columbia* was on course. As they left the moon, the astronauts used up all their remaining photographic film. They must have taken almost a thousand pictures of the moon in the three days they were in its sombre vicinity. As *Columbia* curved around to its 'right' side, they could see the moon gleaming in the sunlight, vividly etched against the black *'It was beautiful,'* wrote Collins, *'but it was nothing compared to earth, and I don't want to come back ever.'*

The trip home was straightforward and incident free. As *Columbia* began to penetrate the thin upper atmosphere of the earth, the sky began to change from the blackness of outer space to a wonderful tunnel of light. They were trailing a comet tail which had a light, orange-yellow centre and blue-green and lavender edges. It grew more intense as the atmosphere became denser, finally expanding so the core of the tunnel became so brilliant that Collins felt he was in the centre of a huge million-watt light bulb. As they entered the atmosphere the spacecraft began to decelerate as it encountered air resistance. A heat shield over its base prevented it from being burnt up (as meteors are) by the friction thus caused.

Their weightlessness began to give way to gravity, gently at first, nudging the astronauts back into their couches, and then began to build up uncomfortably. After eight days at zero gravity, their bodies weren't accustomed to gravity or deceleration. By the time the force peaked at 6.5 G, Collins felt as though a gigantic hand was pushing against his chest. But it didn't last long, and he had other matters to occupy his attention.

Now was the time for *Columbia*'s two small drogue parachutes to open, to slow the spacecraft down sufficiently to release the main parachutes. As the drogues came out, they jerked back and forth, but then the three huge main parachutes replaced them, and *Columbia* was floating down towards what the astronauts hoped was a calm ocean.

They hit the water hard and the command module turned over. Collins threw a couple of switches and rubber bags on *Columbia*'s nose filled with air and turned her the right way up again.

Once they were upright, divers who had been dropped into the ocean by helicopter surrounded *Columbia* and tied a life raft to her side. Then the astronauts opened the hatch, and one of their rescuers threw them three biological isolation suits. These were designed to contain any moon germs. Collins, Armstrong and Aldrin scrambled out of the *Columbia*, and locked the hatch behind them. Once in the raft they washed each other down with disinfectant, just in case any moon germs might be on the outside of their clothes. Then, one by one, they climbed into a wire basket on the end of a cable and were winched up into the helicopter.

Man had finally walked on the moon – and returned to earth alive.

CHAPTER 10

STONE AGE HOSTAGES

Survival is only possible if there is a positive will to survive. Once this is in place, then anything is possible, despite hardship, danger and the daily fear of death.

Bill Oates (23), Daniel Start (23), Anna McIvor (21) and Annette van der Kolk (22) had that will. It was to be sorely tested.

The group had met at Cambridge. All four were scientists. Daniel, who was a neuro scientist, had been the initiator of the expedition as he had always wanted to visit a remote area of Indonesia called Irian Jaya which was unmapped, dense jungle where tribes still live a stone-age life. The students had raised £30,000 to fund the expedition and the Duke of Edinburgh had become its patron. The team also included four Indonesians, Navy Panekenan and his fiancée Adinda Sara Swati, Jualita Tanasale and Yosias Lasamahu, known as Tessy. The expedition was to live in a mission house, built in the jungle by white people who had settled in Mapnduma in the sixties. The scientific group wanted to examine plants and insects of the area as well as birds. They were to be helped by local families and were to gather information never previously available to the West.

The tribes have little concept of the outside world. They live by the rising and setting of the sun and have no logic, entirely relying on instinct, intuition and natural phenomena to guide their thoughts. Few decisions are made. They live in small family groups in the forests and mountains of the area, measuring their wealth in pigs and wives, their only family possession a cooking pot. They wear grass skirts and decorate themselves with feathers. They had originally put tusks through their noses and ears, but since their contact with missionaries they now pierced their noses with ball-point pens instead.

It wasn't until later that the team was made aware of the political situation. The OPM is an underground Free Papua movement which had been causing unrest in the area, and was led by a man known as Kelly Kwalik who had gained a considerable mythical status amongst the natives. The objective of the OPM was to reclaim Irian territory that had been handed over to Indonesia by the United Nations in the early 1960s. They also wanted independence. The expedition members were told, however, not to worry and that as they were white they would not be harmed. In fact, through their scientific work the expedition might be able to help the OPM by raising awareness of the situation. They had a radio which could call up a helicopter within half an hour and the team considered the political situation to be the least significant of their problems; they were far more concerned about someone breaking a leg or becoming ill.

On 8 January 1996, however, a terrifying ordeal began. From the mission house the team watched a hundred naked warriors in black face-paint and feather head-dresses run screaming down a ridge with bows and arrows. Thinking it was a tribal celebration, Daniel reached for his video camera and Bill for his tape recorder. Then they both realized this was not going to be the happiest of occasions. They ran back into the house, yelling warnings to their companions as warriors started heading towards them, locking the doors and listening to their radio being smashed to pieces on the porch.

They then ran upstairs to hide and sat in the middle of the room, away from the windows, suddenly realizing Bill Oates was not with them. But there was no chance of searching for him now as the threatening noise level rose to incredible heights. Two bullets were fired which came through the wooden walls above their heads. The members of the expedition were terrified as they lay on the floor with their arms over their heads, yelling at each other to keep quiet and keep down.

The warriors then began breaking the door down with stones and rocks, circling the house and eventually gaining entry.

Terrible moments of tension followed as they heard the warriors looking for them below. Then they ran up the stairs, trying all the doors until they arrived at the room in which the expedition was hiding.

'*All of us were shaking with fear,*' said Annette. '*We had been living and working with these gentle and peaceful people. We couldn't believe this was happening, so when we heard the voice of one of our workers at the door telling us to come out, we thought he was there to help us, to reassure us that there had been terrible mistake.*'

The only mistake was their trust in the worker, for Daniel Kogoya was a traitor, the undercover commander of the kidnap gang, sent in by Irian freedom fighters. Armed with a Second World War bolt-action rifle, he marched everyone but Bill Oates (who had already hidden himself under his bed) downstairs and on to the front porch. Bill was still running his tape recorder and whispered into it, '*Goodbye – it's been a good life.*' If he survived, his plan was to stay hidden and go for help, but he was soon discovered.

Daniel remembers: '*We were screaming and crying. People were becoming more and more aggressive, throwing bricks into the porch. We thought we might be stoned to death. The warriors behind us were trying to make us move off the porch and into the mob. They shot at our ankles to make us go forward but we were more terrified of what was in front.'*

'I knew that if we went into the mob we would be meat.'

However, help was at hand; local people who had become friends of the scientists formed a human shield to protect them. But they were soon forced to surrender as one tribesman had his hand smashed with a rifle butt, and long machetes were used to threaten protectors and scientists alike.

Finally, the team were pushed out into the open and joined by three other European conservationists from the settlement, including a pregnant Dutch woman, Martha Klein, and her friend Mark Van Wal.

Annette was frightened that they were going to be executed. There was no sense of discipline or organization amongst the warriors who were in a trance-like state, ready for battle. Unfortunately, the expedition seemed to be the enemy.

A shower of rain cooled the tempers of the warriors who had already tied the group's hands behind their backs with vines. Daniel remembered: *'Until then, anything could have happened. It only needed one wrong word to start the killing. But, thank God, it started to rain. We stood in it and watched the steam rising off the warriors.'*

The hostages were marched away from the mission house at Mapnduma by their captors, led by four men who were to act alternately as benign father-figures and cold-blooded killers. These were Daniel Kogoya, whom they later christened Green Beret because of his head gear, Titus Murip, who habitually dressed in green and was therefore dubbed Robin Hood, and Silas Elmin, who they termed Babbay, Indonesian for 'our father', and who always wore a blue balaclava and carried a serrated knife. Despite his unprepossessing appearance, Elmin became both guide and protector to the hostages. Finally there was Doud, who was the most primitive and would go into a trance-like state, hopping from foot to foot, waving a feather fly-switch and wearing a manic grin. The hostages gave him the appropriate nickname of 'Old Nutter'.

All they could hope was for the villagers to somehow get a message out to the authorities, describing what had happened and requesting assistance. As a result, a helicopter would be sent. But this was a lot to expect from such primitive people who, anyway, were in terror of their own lives from the OPM. Frustratingly, there was a plane due at the village, but their captors knew this and made them leave before it came.

They were given little time to make any preparations. For instance, Daniel only had his best orange shirt, a pair of trousers and a suede belt he had been given for Christmas. Everyone's boots had been stolen during the night but he had one pair of shoes. Unfortunately, he forgot to pack any underwear and only had one pair of boxer shorts during his entire captivity.

Fortunately, they were able to write letters which were passed by their kidnappers to local tribes and on to the Red Cross.

Bill wrote to his parents and his girlfriend Kate. *'Sitting round the fire in the chill of a mountain morning you all seem so very far away – I would give anything to be with you all once again. I am living one day at a time; striving to enjoy the simple pleasures and drawing tremendous support from the rest of the group.'*

Some days later, he wrote: *'I always thought I would have my five minutes of fame, but I would rather it was another way! Kate, I think of you every minute and although it hurts, it keeps me strong.'*

The kidnappers were taking them deep into the jungle. The forest was steep, and the ground was so treacherous that they had to think about every step they took. The hostages were ordered to walk in single file while their captors chopped their way through the jungle with machetes. Sometimes they were forced to walk six feet above the ground on tree roots which they could easily have slipped through. Above them was a closed canopy of green which was at least 40 feet (10 metres) high. They knew then they were completely in their captors' control and there was no way of escape. Indeed, they were prisoners of the environment. If they ran they would immediately get lost and, anyway, their captors could easily track them down.

Gradually, as the days became weeks, the hostages realized the full extent of their plight. Their kidnappers believed that western hostages were vital to a free Papua. They also believed that their victims were VIPs from a tribe in England and that their chief would very much want them back. They told the hostages that not only would they remain in the jungle and live with their captors for the rest of their lives, but they would have their children in the wilderness, grow old and die without ever returning home. It was a forbidding statement.

Anna wrote to her parents:

Our moods and morale flip up and down and are quite as unpredictable as the moods of our captors ... I love you all very much, it must be hard for you to imagine our situation, but it is really quite liveable.

I really believe things are in the hands of God, and however things go, it will be for the best.

Courageously, the hostages tried to protect their families from the true knowledge of their sufferings.

In fact their biggest worry was not so much their captors – at this stage anyway – it was a rescue attempt, for if the Indonesian Army did move in they knew there was every chance they would be executed and that the local tribespeople who had become their friends would be in considerable danger.

Yet on a separate level to these threats there was now a strange bonding between the hostages and their captors. Babbay produced a raw and bloodied pig's heart and they were all forced to eat a piece in a darkened hut beside a blazing fire. As they bit into the raw flesh, captors and hostages swore never to harm each other. The ritual was a curious mixture of pagan and Christian practice.

As they were moved from camp to camp, Daniel continued to write home, underlining the strange contrasts of their situation. Terrified by death, or becoming lost for ever in this wilderness, they still felt a peace reflected from their captors' primitive lives.

Yet there were additional dangers, particularly to the women, but Anna and Annette pretended they were married to Daniel and Bill. As the family is sacred to the tribe, this was a sound method of protection.

On the whole, food was reasonably plentiful, but there was a period when the supplies ran out and they were forced to eat forest tubers, baked sweet potatoes, roasted nuts, fruit and the occasional slaughtered pig. Although they lost weight, none of the hostages ever really faced complete starvation.

Annette remembered that at one time they were supposed to be getting a pig – or part of a pig – although this had been promised many times. The thought of pork make them salivate, and the hostages could discuss nothing else.

Later on in their captivity, the hostages were on even shorter rations. They were constantly moving on and spent three weeks on the top of a ridge, a long way from any village, and the food supply simply ran out. As a result they were reduced to two or three potatoes a day, sharing the food democratically, although they all agreed that the Dutch woman, Martha Klein, should get more because she was pregnant. To think of food was sheer torture, and if anyone discussed it, the others had to walk away. They tried to sleep sixteen hours a day so their hunger pangs were more bearable, but at least it provided a bond with their captors who were going hungry too.

Desperation made them inventive, and they ate leaves from sweet potatoes, which tasted like spinach, and scooped out the inside of palm trees which was reminiscent of celery. They boiled ferns, calling the result pond soup, and even ate beetle larvae. Their captors caught frogs and they were given to Martha for protein.

The hostages' only reading matter during this period was an American *Homes and Gardens* and an Australian *Woman's Weekly*. The magazines contained two particularly painful features; one about barbecues, while the other discussed Granny's Biscuit Barrel. Dan memorized the recipes. This was a very bad period when they lost a lot of weight and reached a new mental low.

The support of their families was very precious.

Annette wrote to her parents:

It is amazing how loved one can feel, even in this isolation on the other side of the world.

My dream upon getting out is still to spend a couple of weeks at home with you, going shopping, to the cinema, meeting Dad after work and going to a play, going to Oxford for a day trip, cooking lots and eating lots.

Dan's letter read:

Thank you so much for your letters. They were such a joy and support and I have never cried so much. This is a very hard time, of course, for us all (you as well) but I have learned so much about life from the heartache that I am still happy and strong here.

Later, they met the terrorist leader Kelly Kwalik. He was small but imposing, wearing a fur hat made from the skin of a tree kangaroo. He told the hostages they had been kidnapped because a bishop had told him in a dream that 1996 would be the year his country would be free. He concluded: *'The Lord has sent you. You are the key to a free Papua.'*

Analysing their captors, Bill realized they could never accept individual responsibility so could never make a decision. Their initial reaction to a crisis was to procrastinate. They used no data or logic; everything depended on a feeling or a dream or the signs of the day. The hostages quickly realized that until every single one of the 300 people involved in the OPM agreed, they would never stand a chance of being freed. To counter-balance this grim thought, the hostages knew that at all costs they had to stick together and to gain mental strength through unity.

The more the hostages talked to their captors, the more alien they seemed to become. The terrorists told them the world was very small and the only language was Indonesian. They had only the vaguest concept of other countries, imagining for instance that England is full of big white people who are immensely powerful and have lots of planes. Most worrying of all, they seemed to have heard of Colonel Gaddafi.

Slowly the hostages became used to the fact that time was measured in terms of weeks not days or hours, making their plight stretch to infinity.

Seven weeks later, the hostages discovered that the Red Cross were trying to secure their release, dropping messages from helicopters, and then, on the radio held by their captors, they heard their parents making appeals.

But the OPM had no intention of freeing their valuable hostages unless Papua was liberated, which was ludicrously out of the question.

Some relief came when the Red Cross helicopter brought them a number of packages – clothes, letters and a big parcel of books. There was also a chess board, a pack of cards and Scrabble. At last they were reassured that the outside world not only knew of their situation but were actively trying to do something about it.

At Easter, the hostages tried to convince their captors that they should be released to celebrate the coming Christian festival, but there was no response. By now they were beginning to realize that the OPM was losing control. No progress was being made and its members were getting bored and abdicating responsibility.

Slowly their captors were vanishing. The situation was farcical but still dangerously volatile, and in a moment of despair Daniel felt that they could be prisoners for years and no one would know why they had been captured. Eventually, even their guards might say, *'Well someone knew once, but he has gone home.'*

Meanwhile attempts were being made to secure their release. May 8th was World Red Cross Day and the Red Cross offered the OPM the opportunity to hand over the hostages on this day in a blaze of media attention. A party was duly held in the jungle village where the captives had recently been moved. In order to demonstrate their integration with their captors the hostages put on traditional grass skirts and Bill commented: *'I would have painted myself green and run naked if that was needed to get home.'* As it was, they danced and the male hostages were given tribal arrows to wave in the air and they were forced to hold pigs about to be slaughtered. Instead of granting their release, however, Kwalik got up on the podium and announced war on Indonesia and made himself President of Free Papua. As the Red Cross officials pleaded, he made even more extravagant and impossible demands. Eventually, as the weather deteriorated, the Red Cross helicopter was forced to lift off.

In the end, what the hostages had feared most took place. With the negotiations at stalemate, the Indonesian Army finally moved in, and the predictable blood-letting began. In a calculated attack by their captors, some of the Indonesian hostages were slaughtered, but the Europeans managed to get away and ran for a large river where they knew the army to be camped. When they reached the bank, however, they realized that Anna was missing.

She had been hiding behind a tree as her captors began a search, and crawled under the roots for protection. Anna could distinctly hear one of the dying Indonesian hostages moaning, but she couldn't see him and was too terrified to come out of her hiding place. Nevertheless, she was devastated that she could not help him. Eventually she made her way down a landslide and reached the river.

As she joined her companions, the Indonesian Army moved in on the terrorists and later the hostages were air-lifted out. They had been held for 129 days. Typical of their philosophical courage is this letter:

We have all been very strong. Each day we take pride in finding something beautiful to appreciate and each night take blessing from the fact that we are alive and living. After all, this is an immensely beautiful part of the world and life is a precious miracle. So with these very fundamental things we have been able to take strength, to laugh, joke and generally take life with a pinch of salt ... I hope to be home to see the bluebells. If not, at least to see the summer.

CHAPTER 11

THE HERALD OF FREE ENTERPRISE DISASTER

Zeebrugge is deceptive. Seemingly quite large, this Belgian harbour is in fact three-quarters silted up with mud and sand and there is little room for ships to manoeuvre in and out. Car and passenger ferries are compelled to dock bows first. When a ship departs she has to vacate her berth stern first and then place her stern in a small basin to give her enough room to go ahead into the swept channel between the breakwaters. The manoeuvres are tricky but not demanding.

The *Herald of Free Enterprise* was one of two similar ships of the Townsend Thoresen line, which had just been taken over by P&O who were running a special cheap day excursion to Belgium. She displaced just under 8,000 tonnes and had a capacity for 1,200 passengers. On this occasion the *Herald* was carrying about half this number, but on the return journey she picked up approximately 100 British Army servicemen who were stationed in Germany and going home on leave, together with their families and cars.

Normally, the *Herald* plied between Dover and Calais but on Friday 6 March 1987, one of the other ships in the line was out of service and the *Herald*, sailing early from Dover to Zeebrugge, had undertaken the 2½ hour voyage."

Her return journey was running late when the *Herald* left her berth at 18.30. She took ten minutes to turn, and by 18.42 she was leaving the harbour.

On this home voyage the *Herald* was carrying a number of heavy freight trucks which had been driven on board last. This meant that there was a good deal of weight in her bows, forcing them a little more under water than usual. To make sure that ferries are the right height for their quays, the ships are provided with water ballast tanks, and by flooding or discharging these the height of the bows above the water, and therefore the height of the disembarking platforms, can be varied to suit the tide. Because the bows were lower than usual, it was odd that the bow ballast tanks were not emptied to bring the *Herald* on to a more even keel. This, however, was only one of a series of sloppy practices that had already begun to put the *Herald*, her passengers and crew into imminent danger.

At 18.16, the Belgian Coastguard received an ominous signal from a German coaster who reported that the *Herald* was listing heavily. A minute later, she turned over on her port side; with her upper decks lying parallel to the water and already half submerged she plunged into total darkness.

On board, there was immediate chaos. Those passengers who were sitting in the cafeteria were thrown across to the port side of the saloon and ended up against the plate-glass windows which covered the side of the compartment. They were joined by crockery, glass, hand luggage and furniture. Then the bitterly cold sea came in.

Many people were drowned immediately, whilst the quicker-witted and more resourceful grabbed fittings secured to the deck of the cafeteria, pulling themselves out of the relentless water that was filling the entire area. The lights had gone out and they were in a pitch-black, water-filled pit at the mercy of the ocean and of each other.

The passengers who were not in the bars or the cafeteria were also thrown from one side of the *Herald* to the other, some into the sea itself, most of whom died immediately in the freezing water.

Those on the lower decks stood even less chance of escape and were also drowned, the cross-passages becoming vertical tunnels.

There were few heroes. There rarely are in situations where there is widespread panic. But there were isolated incidents where people showed remarkable, unselfish bravery. Andrew Parker was one of these. He was a 33-year-old bank clerk and had been on the day trip with his wife Eleanor and 12-year-old daughter Janice. When the *Herald* went over they were all three sitting in the lounge, and were thrown across the area together with all the other passengers.

Fortunately for what was to follow, Parker weighed fifteen stone and was 6 foot 3 inches tall. He managed to extricate himself from the screaming pile of passengers and pulled his wife and daughter on to a metal ledge that was still above water. On the other side of the saloon was another ledge from which a broken window offered an escape route to the starboard side, now classified as the 'upper' deck.

Slowly, using his weight and height and strength, Parker pulled some twenty passengers on to the ledge and then he stretched his tall frame across the five-foot gap between ledges and the passengers scrambled over his body and through the broken window. His wife and daughter went too and then he himself.

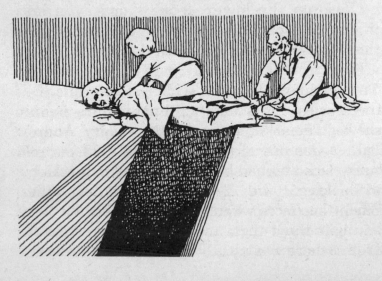

The irony was that the Parkers were all rescued, but in the mêlée they were separated and believed one another drowned, until they were reunited the following morning.

Another hero was a professional soldier – Private Messon of the British Army in Germany who had a spinal injury and was in a wheelchair. His wife was swept away but he managed to secure her clothing with his teeth and dragged her to safety in the wheelchair.

Surviving members of the crew of the *Herald* behaved well by breaking the heavy glass windows on the now upper side of the ship with axes and lowering knotted ropes, taken from the lifeboats, to the passengers on the inside of the windows on the port side of the saloons. Those who had the strength and presence of mind grabbed the ropes and were hauled to safety, although some male passengers knocked women and children off them.

There were other horrendous incidents. In one particular case, a middle-aged man and his wife were battling to stay afloat in one of the water-filled saloons. He was supporting his wife when he saw some men standing on a ledge, talking and smoking. It was very obvious that there was room for one more where they were standing, but when he begged them to help his wife up, they told him there was no room. He pleaded but they ignored him, and soon afterwards his wife slipped out of his arms and drowned.

Dover Coastguard had been quickly informed of the catastrophe and a helicopter arrived from the UK. By 19.00 a huge search and rescue operation was mounted, and soon afterwards five helicopters, a fleet of small craft and two Royal Navy warships were on the scene. The *Herald* was now lying on a sandbank just outside the dredged channel, with a list of about 90 degrees to port. The sandbank had prevented her from turning over completely, and surviving passengers were gathering on the starboard side of the ship which had now become the upper deck.

Most of the passengers were taken off by tugs but there were many more trapped below. The piecemeal rescue also made counting the survivors extremely difficult.

Captain David Lewry had been thrown right across the bridge, injuring his lungs, but he refused to leave the *Herald* until he was told there was nothing else he could do for his passengers – particularly those who had been on the port side and had stood no chance of survival.

Seven Royal Navy divers and twelve Belgian divers were winched on board the *Herald* by helicopter as soon as possible, but they faced an overwhelmingly difficult task, searching in pitch darkness, only able to find the bodies by hand.

The ship was full of mud and sand but what they did find was heartrending – a couple lay in each other's arms, a little girl still held her doll.

But why did the disaster happen? How could a ferry of the *Herald of Free Enterprise* type turn over on a calm night with an eventual loss of 188 lives? The reason was simple, devastating in its carelessness. The bow doors to the car deck had not been closed when the *Herald* had left her berth and the ravenous sea had taken her.

The fact that the bow doors were not closed was indisputably the reason why the *Herald of Free Enterprise* capsized. However this was only one of the 'sloppy procedures' brought to light. The enquiry went on to list:

1 The bridge was not informed if the doors were shut, so the Captain could never be quite sure if anyone had actually checked them.

2 The water in the ballast tank was not pumped out before the ship sailed, making her bows extra heavy. On three separate occasions the Townsend Thoresen management had been given memos from three different captains about this but they had been ignored.

3 It was apparently the Chief Officer's responsibility to see that the bow doors were closed,

but when harbour stations were ordered he had to be on the bridge. It was not possible to be in two places at the same time, but apparently it had not been queried.

4 It was suggested that a warning light on the bridge would be a simple way of ensuring that the Captain knew if the bow doors were still open. It transpired that the management had received a request for one but it had been turned down. A member of the management at first denied they had received such a request, but when questioned he had to admit he had lied.

As a result of this appalling incident, safety procedures on car ferries have now been tightened up considerably, which must be reassuring to all those who make use of them in future.

CHAPTER 12

THE DARIEN GAP

The pan-American highway system is twenty-seven thousand miles long and runs from the snows of Alaska to the deserts of Southern Chile. The system feeds twenty-three nations with both trade and tourism, but clearly poses a threat to the remote wilderness and its peoples as well.

In the middle of the highway, however, there is a blockage, and in December 1971 this blockage was considerable – deep jungle and rivers and swamps and hills that were reminiscent of Conan Doyle's lost world. The Darien Gap. Its length was about two hundred and fifty miles and it was situated at the isthmus of the Darien where the Atlantic almost meets the Pacific. So far the gap had defeated the road engineers.

Major John Blashford-Snell, who was later to found the international adventure training organization Operation Raleigh, was then a professional soldier but better known as an organizer of major expeditions. These had ranged from treks across the North African deserts to the Great Abbai Expedition which made the first descent and scientific explorations of the Blue Nile, and a further expedition to the remote and little known Dahlak Islands of the Red Sea.

Blashford-Snell is an adventurer of the old school, pugnacious, tenacious and unyielding. That was why he was able to cross the Darien

Gap, at that time one of the most dangerous places in the world, forcing Range Rovers and a Land Rover through the jungle with amazing initiative, particularly as the expedition turned out to be the hardest and most frustrating he had ever mounted.

The expedition was to be funded by the British Darien Action Committee, who wanted to drive specially equipped vehicles across the area, thus giving publicity to the need to fill the gap in the road system. Eventually it was decided that Blashford-Snell would lead the expedition and the army gave him leave of absence.

When he approached the Rover Company, they were confident that their Range Rover, powerful brother to the Land Rover, would be the most effective vehicle in such terrain. The expedition was also equipped with an inflatable raft that would carry the two Range Rovers, as well as a couple of Hill Billies, vehicles rather like tracked and motorized wheelbarrows. These were the first to break down and had to be abandoned. The Darien Gap, however, was to be a tremendously difficult task for all the vehicles, and in the end they broke down far more frequently than the human beings. Horses were also included for carrying supplies. They turned out to be rather more reliable than the motorized transport.

A Beaver light aircraft was used for reconnaissance and as it circled the area Blashford-Snell saw that the most prominent trees below were one hundred and fifty feet high, rising out of undergrowth so thick that it looked solid. There was the river, the odd house or village, but no other break in the luxuriant wilderness of vegetation. Eventually, however, Blashford-Snell discovered the best site for a headquarters and the ground planning began. It was decided that the Beaver could be put to a further use. The expedition would carry supplies for two days and then be resupplied by parachute.

At the beginning of the motorized trek, they reached a point near to the Silugandi river. The expedition had already had a tough time, using aluminium bridging ladders on several occasions to get the Range Rovers across ravines. It was hard, hot work, and all the expedition suffered from a raging thirst. By the river, the mud was deep and had been stirred up by the horses, which had overtaken the vehicles when a puncture had brought them to a halt.

Now the jungle proper was beginning, and the canopy of trees prevented the sun from reaching the mud and drying it up. Leaving a man with the vehicle, Blashford-Snell marched on alone to catch up with the horses and their riders, who had set up camp in a small clearing above the

Espave river. The scientific section, who had come up by river from Canitas, were nearby. It was too late in the evening to do repairs to the vehicles and the sappers (engineers), were as exhausted as the other members of the expedition. It had been a hot march of about ten miles, but the participants were still cheerful.

Next morning, the expedition headed into dense jungle and Blashford-Snell paused to gaze back at the sunlit savanna before entering this ominous new world with its enormous trees. Ahead of him was a tunnel of greenery, arched over by tangled growth and hung with trailing vines. The light was now reduced to patches of yellow on the leaf-strewn floor, which produced a remarkable garden of small plants, over which hovered large and beautiful butterflies with iridescent blue wings. Once in the tunnel, the expedition found numerous small creeks and stream beds over which they struggled on slippery rock slabs, or through glutinous mud.

After dark, Blashford-Snell and a colleague continued through the jungle to find the reconnaissance party who were camped on the side of the Bayano river. To reach them, a forty-five minute march was necessary, squelching through thick mud and nearly treading on a huge bird-eating spider (which they resourcefully caught for the scientists). Eventually they reached the recce section's camp which was well organized and tucked deep in the jungle to the side of the trail.

Here they discussed the river crossing. The river was now running very high at three and a half to four mph, but Blashford-Snell was satisfied that they would be able to cross within the next two days. He and his colleagues then returned to their camp on the Espave.

Blashford-Snell saw no reason to avoid church attendance just because he was in the jungle. He began the first of many Sunday services as the tropical night closed in. The sappers were press-ganged into a choir by the promise of free beer, bellowed, 'Guide me O thou great redeemer', and a volunteer read the lesson. Blashford-Snell writes, *'I felt we all have something to be a little proud of ... Already the cry was "On to Bogota". But that was a long way off and first of all we had to conquer two hellishly steep jungle ridges that we had nicknamed the Heartbreak Hills.'*

Blashford-Snell read the prayer of Sir Francis Drake at this particular service: *'Lord God, when thou givest to thy servants to endeavour any great matter, grant us to know that it is not the beginning, but the continuing of the same unto the end, until it be thoroughly finished, which yieldeth the true glory: through him who for the finishing of thy work laid down his life, our Redeemer Jesus*

Christ. Amen.'

Possibly he had forgotten that Drake had died in the Darien. Nevertheless, Blashford-Snell's indomitable spirit supported him through a 'green hell' of shattering proportions.

The logistics of the expedition had been carefully planned, but the wilderness fought back. Black hornets continually attacked them and thorn scratches and tick bites often went septic. At night there were the mosquitoes and the expedition was also threatened by ants, snakes and ferocious wild pigs. The tracks they were using would often collapse or turn into a muddy swamp, so their alloy ladders had frequently to be placed under the tyres of the vehicles.

The night of Tuesday, 25 January 1972, was damp and cold, and they broke camp about ninety minutes after dawn, moving through the jungle in a long straggling column.

On the ground there was a mat of leaves, but there seemed to be no change of season in the jungle, or yellowing leaves as one might see in more temperate climates. Underneath the mat of leaves was a layer of humus from which sprouted thick undergrowth. Visibility was rarely more than twenty yards and the jungle continuously resounded to the drip of the condensing humidity, broken only by the occasional crash of a falling tree.

When the rain came, it came in torrents, turning the tracks into quagmires. The ravines, thick black mud, dense vegetation gulleys, patches of poisonous palms and stinging plants and fast-flowing rivers all seemed to conspire against them, and already some expedition members were finding their sweat-soaked clothes were rotting. On the plus side, the consignment of US Army jungle boots for the expedition were wearing well – *'far superior to the Far Eastern variety that we use in the British Army'*. The remaining Hill Billy's track was continuously clogging up with mud which then set hard in the heat, and needed cleaning out every two hundred metres or

so. They had lightened its load to the minimum, but Blashford-Snell was sure that the machine couldn't go on much longer.

Worse still, the Range Rover swamp tyres couldn't cope with the mud; Blashford-Snell thought of trying tyres of the old road type, but was told that the tread was the same. Wild with frustration, he ordered special chains from the USA to put on the wheels; until they arrived the expedition would have to resort to using ropes.

They heard the Beaver pass overhead once or twice, but the pilot couldn't see any of them beneath the dense jungle canopy.

The sappers, who were highly inventive, had been working at a furious rate on the Range Rovers, and had already lost weight and were looking exhausted. Fortunately, their sense of humour prevailed. Nevertheless, Blashford-Snell was beginning to realize that the task of penetrating the Darien Gap was going to be far more arduous than he had earlier imagined. It might even be impossible.

The next day the reconnaissance party told Blashford-Snell the mud ahead was the worst they had seen so far. As a result, the going was slow.

One expedition member, Phil Church, was ill, with either pneumonia or pleurisy according to the medical officer, probably caused by damaged ribs. He was currently riding in the second Range Rover, and the objective was to get him forward to the next clearing as gently as possible, where Blashford-Snell would radio up a helicopter to take him to hospital. But the mud was becoming an increasing barrier and they had to cut a track through virgin jungle.

As a result of this they became all too familiar with the insect life of Darien. Mosquitoes, gnats and flies attacked them as usual, but there were also inch-long black ants who hated being disturbed. Their bites hurt painfully for hours. Later, the expedition even encountered some stinging caterpillars. The heat and humidity were deeply oppressive and the expedition dripped with sweat. Meanwhile the insects became increasingly vicious. A number of aggressive hornets, living in hollow trees and nests, swarmed out to meet anyone who disturbed them, and within seconds the expedition column would scatter under their attack. There were also inch-wide centipedes and black scorpions and huge spiders, probably of the bird-eating variety, in plentiful and scuttling supply.

When brushing against foliage they picked up bloodsucking ticks which immediately attached themselves to their flesh with such tenacity that they had to be removed by the MO. Snakes, however, although numerous, were usually shy.

There is no doubt about the utter hostility of this area of jungle, as if it was the last bastion of wilderness, determined not to allow the road or its pioneers through. Its attacks were continuous, and often far more subtle than Blashford-Snell could have anticipated.

By cutting a new track the expedition learned an important lesson: trees had to be cut right down to ground level, for as soon as the Range Rovers started on the new trail, they tore out a tyre valve on one of the projecting stumps. To try and achieve more traction, ropes were fitted around the wheels, but unfortunately they twisted and dragged off a brake calibre. The crew was able to replace this, but it was yet another exhausting, heartbreaking frustration. Progress had been slow all day in deep mud, with the sappers using ladders and winching most of the time. Yet the vehicles got to within half a mile of the campsite before the exhausted expedition members stopped for the night and slept where they were. Despite all the difficulties and hardship, the achievements Blashford-Snell's expedition were making had been phenomenal.

They were now camped on the Parti river and next afternoon an FAP (Panamanian Air Force) helicopter arrived with much-needed supplies. It also took the injured man back to base.

The final Hill Billy, which arrived in the late

afternoon, became bogged down in deep mud and its magneto broke. *'The Beaver dropped a spare, but, due to a strange coincidence, Cliff Taylor, the pilot, discovered a man in a green uniform wearing a white hat waving some red cellophane approximately ten miles from us. Understandably he thought it was me and dropped the magneto, some bread and, alas, a supply of pyrotechnics to this strange and, as yet, unidentified figure deep in the jungle.'*

The expedition members were totally exhausted, but in good if ironic humour, despite the mud, the insects and the constantly breaking down equipment and vehicles. The green hell had become permanent.

Blashford-Snell decided to allow his men to stay in camp to recuperate and receive another airdrop; this would enable them to wash their clothes, get the sun to their bodies and take an essential rest.

The expedition had been going for ten days now and its members were exhausted, filthy and bad-tempered. The last Hilly Billy was abandoned and Blashford-Snell rode Cromwell, his powerful bay horse, on through the jungle. Cutting their way through, however, had become increasingly hard and could be likened to cutting through two hundred and fifty miles of giant rhododendron bushes.

To make matters worse, the heavily loaded Range Rovers broke down, and it was later discovered the differential gears had disintegrated. Blashford-Snell gave hasty instructions for the expedition headquarters to contact Rover in England as fast as possible.

Morale had been lowered by the mechanical crisis, and it was decided that while waiting for the parts to arrive the sappers would move forward and try to clear more jungle. As a result, the Range Rovers would have an easier trail to follow. But conditions were still getting worse, and in spite of a long rest the horses were weak and many of them went down in the deep mud. The sappers were as debilitated, showing signs of strain, and one man collapsed at a river crossing.

Was it really lack of morale, or was Blashford-Snell pushing them too hard? He wrote: *'I felt it far better to confide my fears and worries to my horse. To my colleagues I must display confidence and good cheer. For if I seemed dispirited, morale would probably sink even lower.'*

There were two tribes of Indians in the Darien – the Choco and the Cuna. The Choco were stocky, with sharp features, and both men and women were naked to the waist. They tended to live in isolated family groups in the valleys and were more friendly than the Cuna.

Although the Cuna were rather less primitive, they kept themselves apart. The men wore jeans and western-style shirts whilst the women wore an elaborately patterned blouse called a *molla*. The Cuna were small, wiry, and lived in large villages on the higher ground. Blashford-Snell decided to hire some of the Cuna to supplement his own exhausted men and he went to the village of Ipeti to bargain with the Cuna elders.

'Travelling silently upstream in the dark, propelled expertly by two young braves, we were greeted by others at the entrance to the village and taken up to the council chamber.' As they entered the low building, they could make out glimmering candles set on small tables. Here sat the women of the village, embroidering and also smoking pipes; children scampered about the floor, and on tiered seats sat the men of the village. In the centre of the room was a long bench with two hammocks set at right angles to it. In one of these hammocks swung the chief and his deputy. Blashford-Snell's interpreters sat on the right and he and his two companions self-consciously joined them.

After the customary formal greetings, Blashford-Snell began to ask questions through his interpreters – a slow procedure because everything they said had first to be translated from English into Spanish then from Spanish to Cuna. Blashford-Snell learnt the chief was democratic, putting any major decisions to the vote of the entire village.

Later, they learned that they had been able to hire twenty men, at a good price of $1.50 per man per day. The chief asked them how he and his comrades would communicate with the people who could speak no English or Spanish. He was nonplussed for a moment, but then said, 'Ah, but I have a Gurkha!'

'How prudent,' said the chief, not understanding what a Gurkha was.

The chief then asked Blashford-Snell many questions about the expedition and also asked him to design an airstrip, 'which I did on the back of an envelope'. Like Baden-Powell, Blashford-Snell's motto must always have been 'be prepared'.

The chief was anxious that his people should become educated as quickly as possible. He also confided that he was concerned about the Bayano Dam which had been built near Canitas, and what would happen to his hunting grounds and his village if the lake spread up the Ipeti River.

Well pleased with the meeting, Blashford-Snell returned to camp, noticing again how unsettling the jungle could be at night as its creatures returned to hunt and feed. Monkeys screamed, frogs croaked, and at river level, by the light of his torch, red eyes glowed from the bank as small caymans waited expectantly in the shallows.

The Indian workers sadly deserted on the first day of their employment, one of them having been bitten by a horse. Blashford-Snell thought this was only an excuse as *'Randy* (the stallion) *bit everyone and it wasn't a very bad bite.'*

Whilst still waiting for the Range Rovers to be repaired, he acquired an older and battered Land Rover. Maybe this would do the job where its much more modern counterparts had failed. Blashford-Snell planned to put the vehicle up front, trail-blazing for the remaining two, which he hoped would arrive soon with fully effective repairs. Eventually the Range Rovers were fixed up with new differentials, but by 4 March these had broken up again and the engineers could only suggest that it might help if the load was reduced by 15 per cent. They also suggested a capstan should be used on every slope. The ladders on the roofs of the Range Rovers, which weighed about one hundred pounds each, might also be causing the trouble, for a high load sets up severe torque on the back axle as the vehicle goes up a slope. Blashford-Snell grimly knew they were going to have a tricky time getting them to Santa Fe, as well as now having a shortage of drinking water. But when weren't there difficulties on this amazing expedition?

Eventually an engineer was flown out from England to effect more repairs.

It soon became necessary to continue the tortuous journey by raft, over a sponge-like terrain that was rapidly filling with water, but a few kilometres ahead was a low, grass-covered embankment that would eventually carry the pan-American highway. The Land Rover had got there first, and one of the Range Rovers was slowly and painfully heading in that direction, slipping and sliding on the muddy surface. The vehicle was helped along by the sappers, their bodies covered in bites, cuts and sores, their trousers filthy with mud.

Returning from making arrangements with the authorities to greet the expedition's success, Blashford-Snell arrived at the rendezvous – a school in Barranquillito. It was 01.30 hours and he discovered the first Range Rover already there, surrounded by exhausted, sleeping men. For better or worse, the Darien Gap had been crossed.

CHAPTER 13

SHOT DOWN IN THE DESERT

"A British Tornado fighter-bomber has been lost during raids on Iraqi targets, according to military sources in the Gulf quoted by the Press Association national news agency.

The agency said it was understood to be the first loss among seventy-five British warplanes in the region in Thursday's fighting.

The precise location of the incident and the fate of the two crew were unknown.

The aircraft was engaged in a second wave of daylight raids after the initial attacks under cover of darkness."

17 January, 1991. REUTERS NEWS SERVICE

The RAF Tornado ground attack aircraft was doing 620 mph above the Iraqi desert. Deployed in Operation Desert Storm during the Gulf War in 1991, the pilot was John Peters, with navigator John Nichol.

Travelling at twice the speed of sound, the SAM-16 missile, its infra-red warhead locked relentlessly on to the furnace heat of the aircraft's engines, found the jet's tailpipe, piercing the heart of its right turbine. The titanium-laced high explosive vaporized on impact, blowing the thirty-ton aircraft sideways.

The Tornado had only just completed an attack on the Ar Rumaylah airfield in southwestern Iraq and Peters was putting the aircraft through a hard turn.

'We've been hit,' yelled Nichol.

Normally, in peacetime, crew would eject from an aircraft with only one engine on fire, but in wartime, especially over enemy territory, it is considered safer to fly on in the hope that the fire might burn itself out. Each of the Tornado's engines sits in a titanium shell which, theoretically, should allow the fire to do just that. Modern aviation fuel won't catch fire easily, and there is usually little problem flying on one engine.

Although both men knew they would not be able to refuel in mid-air, they thought they had a chance of reaching a reserve airfield, or of 'banging out' (ejecting from the aircraft) over friendly Saudi Arabian territory.

However, they soon realized that the extent of the fire in the Tornado, mainly centred in the tail and on the right wing, was far greater than they had imagined. Peters wanted to give the order to eject, but Nichol told him to wait until he had worked out their exact location. They were currently over featureless desert, but Nichol was able to radio in their exact position to his formation leader, hoping that one of the large Special

Forces Black Hawk helicopters would be winching them up from the desert floor in a few hours' time, while Apache gunships and fighter cover kept the Iraqis at bay.

Before ejecting, Nichol called up the formation leader again and described their situation succinctly: *'We are on fire! We have got to come out. We are ejecting. Ejecting.'*

Peters pulled the stick back and called to Nichol, *'Prepare to eject, prepare to eject... Three, two, one. Eject! Eject!'*

They both pulled hard at the handles between their legs and heard a faint mechanical thud. Restraining straps whipped round them, drawing their arms and legs firmly against the frame of the seat. After what seemed like an endless and nerve-scorching delay, the ejector rockets fired.

At thirty times the force of gravity, Nichol and Peters were tossed high into the air with a deafening wind rush and a roaring sound from the seats' rocket motors. They began to turn over and over, all too conscious of the crushing slipstream of at least 400 mph. Peters afterwards wrote: *'Try putting your hand out of the car window at seventy miles per hour, then multiply that sensation by a factor of six. There is a feeling of falling, endlessly falling, somersaulting end over end.'*

Eventually the drogue gun fired out a small, stabilizing parachute to slow up the process, and

as their seats came upright their main parachutes were deployed. There was a jarring crack
as the canopy snapped open and a massive jerk
as it took their weight.

At last, Peters and Nichol were safe in the air.
But the air was the only place they could be safe,
as they were drifting down towards enemy territory.

As he descended, Nichol watched the Tornado
crash in a huge ball of red flame, swiftly followed
by dense black smoke – a significant advertisement of their presence.

At the moment, however, they both wanted to
concentrate on landing, always the trickiest part
of a parachute descent. One of their colleagues
had broken both his legs in a previous ejection in
the UK, entirely because he hadn't lowered his
pack before impact. To ensure a safe landing, it
was essential to pull the release strap so that the
pack hits the ground first. Desperately fumbling
at the pack release straps, Peters and Nichol just
managed to get rid of their loads before they
landed.

Nichol fell on his backside, winded, and Peters,
coming to earth some hundred yards away,
received a cut over his left eye.

Looking round the brown wastes of the desert,
both suddenly and surprisingly began to laugh
uncontrollably. Apart from the giveaway of the
burning Tornado, they could not have cut a more

obvious sight with their flying and biological war-fare suits, life-jackets, helmets, water bags, and packs. Their parachutes were billowing on the ground and, to make matters even worse, to get their personal location beacons out, Peters and Nichol had to inflate their Day-Glo orange life jackets. John Nichol wrote: *'Perfect camouflage, of course: about as unnoticeable as a pack of baboons Christmas shopping on Oxford Street.'*

Once the beacons were out, he started trans-mitting that they were both down and alive in the Iraqi desert. He gave the bearing and hoped the helicopter would come soon. Nichol also hoped the signals were not being received by the enemy.

The survival box, made of bright yellow fibre-glass for identification at sea, was ludicrously all too obvious in the desert. The box held dinghies (Day-Glo orange), separate haversacks with water, food, extra clothing and survival knives. Unfortunately, the method by which the kit was packed meant Nichol and Peters were forced to inflate the dinghies. Helplessly, and beginning to shake with laughter again, they watched the inflatables loom out of their packs. The sight was ridiculous. It was also incredibly dangerous.

Suddenly they both realized something that was most disquieting and their laughter died away. There had been no warning on the RHWR

(Radar Homing and Warning Receiver) and no visual sighting of the missile. It had swarmed up from behind, having been launched from the ground, rather than swooping down on the Tornado from the air. This meant that the troops who had shot them down were nearby and were probably even now searching for them, and attention would be all too easily drawn to the brightly coloured display that was making the aircrew such sitting targets.

They quickly deflated the life jackets with Peters' Swiss Army penknife and buried them in the sand. They then stabbed and slashed at the dinghies until they could also be at least partially buried.

Peters and Nichol then put on their haversacks, checked their pistols and began to move away from the debris of equipment they had left behind. Nichol soon noticed, however, that Peters seemed to have damaged his leg as well as his eye and was limping badly.

The surface of the desert was deep and treacherous and they could only move forward at a shuffle. To add to their misery, the sun was incredibly hot and their flying gear made them sweat and quickly become dehydrated.

Nichol pointed out that they were leaving telltale tracks behind them, and suggested they went down on their hands and knees.

Their exhausted hilarity grew when Nichol realized he was still carrying a route map and tried to eat a section of it. He buried the rest in the desert sand.

He remembered that the still slightly muzzy Peters had been given a list of useful Arab phrases by a member of the British Club in Bahrain. He pulled the piece of paper out of his flying suit and they read it over together. At first, the list seemed innocent enough:

I am hurt, can you help me?

Pilot, need food, please give me water.

May the peace of God be with you.

Then the list became rather more eccentric and later downright insulting, underlining the compiler's unfortunate sense of humour:

I did enjoy the dried breadcrumbs and water. You really must give me the recipe before I leave.

Yes, Your Excellency, travelling in the boot of your car would be fine.

Right at the bottom of the sheet there was the comment:

Saddam Hussein is a bastard. I hate him.

Once again, a burial was made in the sand.

Nichol and Peters walked for an hour, feeling increasingly uneasy. Then they heard a sudden noise, and flattened themselves against the ground. The sound faded away but they still lay there. After a while they began crawling across the sand on their stomachs, although Peters' leg was stiffening and his eye swelling.

Soon they were both sure they could see movement in the south, and it wasn't long before they could make out an armoured personnel carrier coming towards them. Then a group of figures began to shimmer on the horizon.

Again they flattened themselves against the ground as a red pick-up truck drove past their position several times, less than half a mile away. A volley of shots rang out and the mirage-like images became a skirmish line which was advancing, searching diligently.

More shots were fired and both Peters and Nichol realized they were being flushed out. Neither of them had ever been shot at so close to, and the effect was terrifying, especially as they could see the search party had powerful AK-47 automatic rifles.

Now Nichol could see at least twelve of the patrol, all with automatic weapons. They wouldn't stand a chance. Very slowly, they got to their feet with their arms raised. Immediately they hit the ground again as hard as they could. The enemy was firing at them, charging towards their position, screaming. When they stopped firing, Nichol and Peters stood up, hands raised – and then threw themselves flat as the firing started up all

over again. It was farcical, but this time neither of them laughed.

The Iraqi officer shouted in English: '*Stop! Give yourselves in!*' Nichol suddenly realized that in the chaos the Iraqis had thought they were firing back at them. Both men stood up, trembling, and this time there was no more firing.

The Iraqis grabbed Peters' gun and Nichol's radio. There were three Bedouin trackers, a boy of about twelve and a number of uniformed airmen from Ar Rumaylah, the base that had been shot up by the other Tornados. Furiously angry, a Bedouin in traditional robes came up to Nichol, yelling and then punching him in the face. Fortunately for them both, an officer intervened or Nichol might have been beaten to death.

The Iraqis took everything, including £1,000-worth of survival money in gold sovereigns that Nichol had on him. An Iraqi lieutenant also removed his flying watch, telling him not to worry and that he would give it back later. Nichol realized the chances of its return were slender. But so was their survival.

The Iraqis tied both men's hands behind their backs and herded them into the red pick-up truck. The Bedouin boy was enormously elated and waved his hands in the air. The Iraqi lieutenant told them, *'He is very excited. You came from the skies.'*

They then drove Peters and Nichol back to where they had landed, and they grimly realized that although they had been walking in the desert for two to three hours, the truck took less than three minutes to get back. They had only made half a mile's progress.

Nichol's final image of the Bedouin was the young boy on the back of the truck with a gun in his hand, repeatedly drawing his finger across his throat. His gestures were not reassuring. RAF Flight Lieutenants John Peters and John Nichol were badly tortured and battered almost beyond recognition by their Iraqi interrogators. They were later shown across the world on Iraqi television.

Fortunately, they survived the appalling experience, to be released at the end of the Gulf War when Saddam Hussein finally surrendered.

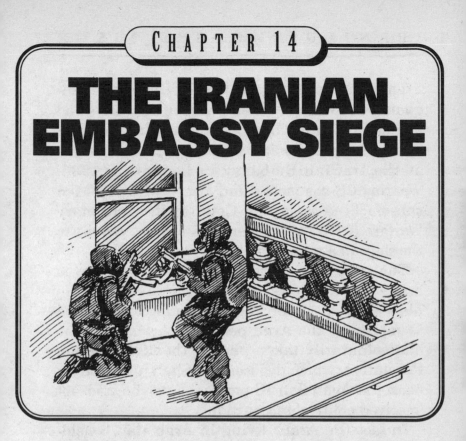

CHAPTER 14

THE IRANIAN EMBASSY SIEGE

Survival in military terms requires detailed planning, total decisiveness and adaptability to situations that are volatile. A siege has refinements; the hostage takers need to be 'talked down', and, where possible, a voluntary surrender is to be encouraged. Alternatively, the talking down must lull the hostage takers into a false sense of security until a surprise raid enforces the surrender or killing of those inside. Unless the latter is extremely well managed, the hostages, or at least some of them, will also die.

The recent siege of the Branch Davidian head-quarters at Waco in Texas was long but in the end botched, with carnage as the result. A classic example of a successful conclusion to a siege was at the Iranian Embassy in London in 1980. Wearing CS gas masks and armed with HK MP5 sub-machine guns, the Counter Revolutionary Warfare (CRW) team members of the SAS broke the siege in a minutely planned operation.

The take-over of the Iranian Embassy was made by a group calling themselves the Mahealdin Al Naser Martyr Group who claimed to represent the Arab people of Arabistan who had voluntarily taken part in the 1979 Iranian Revolution, which deposed the Shah and brought back the Ayatollah Khomeini, but who had not 'received political recognition'.

In fact the Arabs living in Arabistan considered that they had been subject to even more oppression under the Ayatollah Khomeini than the former deposed Shah. As a result, many young men and women joined a relatively new political group called the Arab People's Political Organisation.

The Mahealdin Al Naser Martyr Group, who had the same sympathies, made its demands clear from the start of the seige.

1. The release of 91 young Arabs held in Arabistan.

2. A plane to fly them from Tehran to London.

3. Transport to take all hostages from the Embassy to Heathrow Airport.

4. Safe passage to fly the released prisoners, hostages and gunmen to an undisclosed country in the Middle East.

5. The recognition of Arabistan and the granting of autonomy to the region.

If these demands were not met, then the group of six gunmen claimed they would blow up the Embassy and all those inside the building. They had chosen London for the seige as they knew this would give their cause international recognition.

The building itself had fifty rooms and twenty-two hostages, and when the SAS were finally called in on the sixth day, fifteen men were in Room Ten, which contained telex equipment, and was on the second floor overlooking the street. They were guarded by three terrorists. Five additional women hostages, all members of the Embassy staff, were being held by one terrorist only in Room Nine, on the opposite side of the building across a landing.

BBC reporter Sim Harris, in the Embassy by chance to obtain a visa, and PC Trevor Lock, attached to the Diplomatic Protection Group, were near the telephone on the first floor landing with Oan, the leader of the group, as he negotiated with the police. To rescue all these scattered groups was a considerable problem for the SAS, and as the police continued to negotiate and the SAS to plan, Oan threw down the gauntlet by shooting the Iranian press attaché, Shaheed Abbas Lavasani, and dumping his body on the steps at Princes Gate. Oan also threatened to shoot another hostage in 45 minutes unless his demands were met.

By now the police were convinced it was even worse than that. On their monitoring equipment they had overheard the gunmen planning to kill everyone by 10 p.m. that night.

The SAS had to go in. Planning time had run out.

The team intended to get into the Embassy by abseiling down from the roof, although the operation did not go as smoothly as they had hoped. There were also considerable hazards. The only possible assault route at the front of the building was across a first-floor balcony and through a window of armoured glass which would have to be blown in.

The element of surprise was essential, but was more difficult to achieve because Own and his group were prepared for an attack.

The SAS had decided to work in two teams, with four pairs of men beginning their descent on two ropes down the back of the building while another team, armed with frame charges of plastic explosive to blow in the front window, were stationed on an adjoining balcony.

Unfortunately, when the first abseil team began the descent one soldier accidentally swung at an upper-storey window and smashed it with his boot. The sound of breaking glass rang through the building and Own replaced the telephone on which he was talking to the police negotiator and went to investigate, followed by PC Lock.

Own had in fact made a bad miscalculation, one so simple and yet so disastrous that it could have destroyed all his chances. Perhaps he had assumed the traditional British bobby wouldn't be armed. In this case, however, he was wrong. PC Lock had kept on his full uniform, top coat included, throughout the siege. The reason for this was that he *was* armed – with a .38 revolver – and he was waiting for an opportunity to use it. With this in mind he didn't let Own out of his sight.

Because of the kicking-in of the window, the original SAS plan had to be changed. Originally, the abseil teams at the rear of the building had planned to wait until the front team had blown out the window. Now they had to move right away.

An electronic camera a TV news company smuggled into position caught the amazing speed of the rear team's descent. As the first pair down prepared to blast their way into the Embassy, the second pair had gained the rear first-floor balcony, smashing the window and throwing through it a stun grenade. But disaster struck again when one of the next pair became trapped on his abseil rope and was completely stuck, unable to move up or down.

If the ground-floor pair set off the explosives, there was little doubt they would kill him. Instead, they made the decision to follow the example of their colleagues above, smashing the windows and hurling in the stun grenades.

As one of the SAS team entered the building he faced Own levelling a gun at him. He would have been killed had it not been for the courageous action of PC Lock who brought the terrorist down with a rugby tackle. As they struggled, Lock pulled out his pistol, but the SAS soldier told him not to fire. Own rolled clear, pointing his gun at Lock, but was killed by a burst of fire from the SAS team member's sub-machine gun.

Meanwhile, in the front of the building, everything was still going to plan as two SAS soldiers were busy placing an explosive charge over the window. Two minutes after the rear team had begun their attack, a large explosion destroyed the armour plated glass and the team ran into the room through the smoke and up the stairs.

There they met Sim Harris trying to reach the balcony through a front window. They yelled at him to get down as a cartridge of CS gas was fired from outside the building into a room at the top of the Embassy where a sixth terrorist was hiding.

There was less resistance amongst the remaining terrorists who were holding the hostages. When the group were evacuated from the Embassy and held on the lawn they were all bound in case any of the gunmen were sheltering amongst them. A police marksman, who had seen the terrorist earlier, looking out of the Embassy window, alerted the SAS, and although one of the women hostages tried to protect him he was soon identified by Sim Harris.

Three terrorists guarding Room Ten panicked and began to shoot their hostages, killing assistant press attaché Samad-Zadeh and then trying to kill Dr Gholam-Ali Afrouz, the chargé d'affaires.

As the SAS approached the room, how-ever, the terrorists again pretended to be hostages, but one of the real hostages pointed them out.

Finally, the last remaining terrorist, who had locked himself in one of the rooms was killed. This was the first time the SAS had carried out an operation on British soil, and if the attack had gone wrong they would have lost an enormous amount of credibility. Fortunately, due to the quick and flexible decisions of this highly trained and dynamic team of soldiers, the ending of the siege had been successfully brought about, and most of the hostages survived unharmed.

CHAPTER 15

THE
EXPEDITION
THAT
FAILED

On 22 February 1994, an army adventurous training expedition under the command of Lieutenant-Colonel Robert Neill began to explore Low's Gully on Mount Kinabalu in northern Borneo. There were ten soldiers in the team, but within a couple of days five of them had become separated from the main group and the expedition turned into a disaster, with Neill and his second-in-command, Major Ron Foster, together with three Hong Kong soldiers, stranded in the wilderness depths of the gully. After the successful rescue of the expedition, a Board of Inquiry was held.

Robert Neill, the son of a Gloucester doctor, was 46 at the time of the expedition, a Sandhurst graduate and Ron Foster was his social opposite; he had left Barton Grammar School with six 'O' levels, eventually joining the Ordnance Survey as a cartographical draughtsman and surveyor, and then the army. Both men had a love of outdoor pursuits and both were fascinated by Mount Kinabalu and had been on expeditions to it before. At the time of the 1994 expedition, Neill was still in the army but Foster was a member of the Territorial Army.

Low's Gully is an immensely deep ravine which plunges down the north side of Mount Kinabalu. The gully, covered in dangerous jungle, is hostile and inaccessible – one of the last great untouched wildernesses left on earth.

In 1851, Sir Hugh Low, British Colonial Secretary, together with forty Dusun porters, had found himself gazing down into *'a circular amphitheatre... the bottom of which, from its great depth and my position overhanging, was indiscernible.'*

He was not in a position to go any further, for the Dusun believed that the peak of the mountain was inhabited by a dragon which lived in a cave, guarding a huge jewel, and that the top of the mountain was covered with precious stones (probably hailstones) that no one was allowed to touch. The Dusun also told Sir Hugh Low that when the Chinese first visited the mountain they infuriated the dragon by stealing its fire. As a result the dragon cursed all Chinese and those who tried to explore the mountain were lured to their deaths. Ironically, Neill's expedition contained three Hong Kong Chinese soldiers.

After considerable climbing practice the 1994 expedition was ready to make the descent, though they too found the sight of the gully both imposing and threatening. A huge amphitheatre, over half a mile across, was spread below them with a 40-degree slope of exposed light-grey rock that fell sharply beneath their feet and swept away to the right. In the middle of the bowl primeval boulders rose to sheer cliffs and the peaks which bounded the valley on the far side. The sight was as disturbing as it was desolate, and it was with considerable apprehension that the expedition descended into a still wilderness with no birdsong, nor the stirring of any living creature, however small.

The unexpected length of the descent and the difficulty of the terrain, together with a seriously misremembered communication between Colonel Neill and Private Mayfield, who was in charge of the reconnaissance group, were the main reasons why the expedition became split, also rapidly running out of rations. The situation was further complicated by the fact that Neill picked up a virus and for a short while Foster had to take command, although Neill soon recovered to lead further major abseils (a controlled descent on a rope over vertical or very steep drops) down a gully that began to seem endless.

From the first, Neill was worried by the slowness of the progress they were making. The expedition only had enough rations for six days and he soon became aware that they would need at least one more day to reach their objective.

On Day 6, Tuesday, 1 March 1994 they finally emerged from a wood and saw the floor of the gully at last. Huge boulders littered the bed of the watercourse, and the granite cliffs rose sheer for 2300–2600 feet (7 – 800 metres).

Unfortunately, however, a huge waterfall and cliff fell away below them and Neill realized that the reconnaissance group that had already split away from them would have needed all their ropes to abseil down it and would therefore not have been able to get back up. Had they in fact gone down? Or pulled back at the last moment? If so, why hadn't they reported to Neill?

He knew that his own group would have to continue on down, although it was increasingly difficult to manage without Mayfield, who was the rock-climbing expert. In fact it took six separate abseils to descend the 327 yard (300 metre) drop.

Then, disastrously, the weather changed; mist came up from below them and rain began to fall. Instantly Neill realized how forbidding the gully had become. The surface of the boulders became incredibly slippery, and the chances of injury tripled. In fact, movement was so difficult that their progress became negligible.

Neill knew his group had to find shelter fast, and as there was no possible chance of pitching a tent, they began to look for a boulder with an overhang.

Next day, progress was even slower and injuries, small but annoying, began to mount. By the end of Day 9, the level of water was rising dangerously in the gully and the roaring of the waterfall was becoming oppressive.

On Day 10 the real horrors of the gully were beginning to make themselves felt as the steep sides narrowed down to a V-shaped channel that was scarcely more than a yard wide at its base, with the smooth rock faces rising sheer from the water, black and glistening for the first 10 yards or so, and then covered with vegetation. Below lay two narrow pools along the bed of the ravine, steel grey under a cloudy sky, the second on a level lower than the first. Above the start of the first pool, a single boulder was wedged in the foot of the rock V, with water cascading over it. The far end of the pool was blocked by a second boulder. Beyond it the gully vanished. As Neill put it, *'We were looking at air.'*

At this point the two officers considered their position and decided that it would be foolhardy to continue further into the gully. The weather was against them; even if they managed to get down they definitely would not be able to get back again, and much-needed equipment – not to mention expertise – was with Mayfield's party. The three Hong Kong soldiers were relieved to hear their decision and the entire party attempted to find their way back. The torrential rain, however, made even retreat impossible and they were overjoyed when Kevin Cheung chanced upon a cave. Unable to go up or down, Kevin's cave became their base for the next three weeks.

Foster summed up the reasons for staying where they were in his journal:

a) *Water too dangerous to carry on.*
b) *Hong Kong soldiers need rest.*
c) *Several minor injuries.*
d) *Any escape bid must be planned properly in view of our failed attempt yesterday.*
e) *Conserve energy and rations.*
f) *We are by water.*
g) *We have shelter.*
h) *Liew said helicopters available.*
i) *We can be seen from the air.*
j) *This is the most suitable spot in this part of the gully for a helicopter to get in.*

As the expedition was already two days late for their return to Park Headquarters they hoped that the Malaysians would soon begin to search for them. Neill and Foster had also arranged to meet Robert New, a local climber, for a drink on the evening of Tuesday, 8 March. Surely he would raise the alarm if they didn't arrive?

The next morning, Monday, 7 March, the rain stopped and the sun came out, making the five men much more optimistic.

Taking advantage of the better weather conditions Neill and Foster set out flat grey stones on a base of thick green moss to spell out the letters SOS. The message stood out well. Foster also made a figure 5 out of stones so that any helicopter would recognize there were five people. He also laid out his emergency spare blanket, made of aluminium, which would flash in the sun, and Neill displayed his red equipment sack.

Neill was obsessed with the fate of the first group. Could they have been washed away? Had they survived? He felt 'gutted', overwhelmed by his responsibilities. The expedition down into the gully had been his idea and he felt he had underestimated its dangers. His current idea was to recover strength, conserve energy, wait for the weather to improve and then try to escape from the gully.

One of the main problems was, of course, the dwindling rations, and these had to be eked out. As a result, the expedition was getting increasingly low in protein.

Neill was also concerned that his men should stay dry in case of hypothermia, although one blessing was that there was no wind, only still air, and therefore the expedition was less prone to heat loss.

Next morning, armed with a knife he borrowed from Private Chow, one of the Hong Kong soldiers, Neill went out on a long reconnaissance, cutting blazes on both sides of the bark of selected trees. As he explored the terrain, Neill was delighted to find evidence that the first reconnaissance group had managed to climb out of the gully. Under the roots of a tree were discarded clothes, ration wrappers and a sleeping bag in bad condition.

Later, however, he began to see that he was not going to find an escape route and was about to return to camp when a branch gave way and he fell, hitting his head. For a moment, a deadly panic swept him as he realized his sense of direction had entirely disappeared – as had his compass. The rain had returned, the waterfalls seemed to fill his head and Neill had never felt so utterly and completely defeated.

Eventually he found the blazes and made it back to the cave but he would never forget the horror of being lost in the wilderness of the gully.

But on Friday, 11 March, with the weather fine and looking like holding, Foster and Neill decided to have another try at finding an escape route.

All the soldiers were now in poor physical shape. None of them were in a fit enough state to explore the gully, and it was essential that some members of the party stayed behind in charge of the SOS and to tell any rescue party where the others were.

After three hours of climbing, Neill and Foster were halted by a rock slab that was completely impassable. Eventually Foster found a possible route, but it led down towards the south, which was the direction they least wanted to take.

They bivouacked that night and then on the morning of 12 March, Foster and Neill continued up the side of the gully, although the going was becoming increasingly treacherous.

Their route was dangerously steep and they were forced to hang on to bushes, orchids, branches, roots and grass. The thick layer of loose, wet moss over rock made walking a slippery, sliding process. Neill almost slipped into a miniature ravine, but the foliage prevented his fall.

They debated whether to go back or not and Foster pressed Neill to make one more effort. Neill, however, was all too conscious that if one of them became injured, then there would be a dire responsibility for the other. Eventually, they were stopped in their ascent by a vertical bank of soil and mud and even Foster had to admit defeat.

The next morning they were overjoyed to hear the sound of a helicopter and then see it circling far out to the north, somewhere over the Penataran River. They watched the helicopter fly across the opening of the gully and tried to attract the attention of the pilot. Foster fired the flash gun of his camera and they both laid out a red equipment sack, mess tins and any other shiny object they could lay their hands on.

The helicopter disappeared from view but they

were both hopeful that it might return. Had the aircraft been looking for them, or had it been commissioned for some other purpose? Neill and Foster were determined to keep optimistic, particularly as they knew they now had to report back to the Hong Kong soldiers that they still had not found an escape route.

They spent the daylight hours reorganizing the cave and packing their kit, once again optimistically hoping for the arrival of a helicopter. Meanwhile, their physical deterioration continued. Foster and Neill tried to pass their time by playing chess. They all talked about their families, interests, careers and ambitions until each member of the expedition began to know the others intimately. The rest of the time they dwelt on their twin obsessions: the whereabouts of the reconnaissance party and the possibility of an organized rescue. Surely a search must be in operation by now?

On 16 March, Foster heard a whistling sound and thought the torrents of water were returning. Instead, a huge rock came hurtling towards him, followed by four others. They crashed into the cave, and at first Foster thought there would be fatalities. Fortunately, only Chow was slightly hurt. Nevertheless, it did seem as if the gully was unleashing its forces against them. Observing his companions, Foster wrote in his journal: *'They all look very thin. I suppose I do too. Always wanted a thirty-two inch waist. Now I've got a twenty-eight! Kevin is in Chow's bag to try and dry it, and Chow is in Kevin's to keep warm.'*

Heartbreakingly, they were soon engulfed in another flood, more powerful this time, and they were wet through in seconds.

By 18 March, the weather had cleared again and they took turns on chopper watch, scanning the skies, wondering what on earth had happened to their rescuers. It was a thought that possessed their minds twenty-four hours a day, even in sleep.

That day, the only food available was a biscuit each and the last of a packet of chicken soup. Now all that was left were some glucose tablets,

a few drink-powders, some sachets of beef stock, a tin of meat paste and four biscuits. There was no natural food in the gully; the plants were very likely to be poisonous. Unless help came soon, they would slowly starve to death.

On Saturday, 19 March, Foster, bigger and more heavily built than the others, decided to make one last attempt to escape from the now deadly trap of the gully. Before departing he made some final preparations in case the worst happened – and found that everyone else had much the same idea. He gave out some paper so the Hong Kong soldiers could write notes and wills. The Chinese had voluntarily reduced to one biscuit a day earlier on, so they still had some rations. Raiding the medical box, Neill found half a packet of glucose tablets and Foster found throat pastilles and stomach tablets and Diarolyte (replacement salts). They looked on them as rations.

Foster set off on the morning of 20 March, and used up the last ounces of his strength in his desperate reconnaissance on a 70-degree slope. He somehow struggled his way up through areas choked with vegetation which were ominously full of the thick, musky smell that often pervades undisturbed forest. Eventually, having worked his way to the far side of the watercourse, he came to the base of yet another cliff.

Foster bivouacked by a moss-covered waterfall course, and despite his incredible feat of exertion he didn't collapse into a deep sleep but had a disturbed and restless night.

On 21 March, as Foster woke to a feeling of helplessness and Neill to severe depression, a dull green military helicopter roared into view, flying high. Neill saw the aircraft as he emerged blearily from the cave. Foster saw it just as he had recovered a foothold after dangling a hundred yards above the rocks when a patch of moss on which he had been standing gave way.

The appearance of the helicopter gave him an incredible shock, and Foster began firing his camera flash, as well as setting out his space blanket and equipment sack. The aircraft gave the impression of searching, but it didn't come up the gully itself, which made Neill suspect that its appearance had nothing to do with them at all. It was not a suspicion, however, that he wanted to spread around.

That afternoon Foster rejoined them, and the next morning all five men were awake early and listening out for the slightest sound. Then they heard it – the unmistakable, unbelievable sound of an approaching helicopter. When the aircraft came into view, they could see it was flying high and seemed not to have any particular purpose in passing over the gully. Kevin fired the camera flash and

Victor flashed SOS in Morse code with his torch.

For a glorious moment, Foster thought they had been spotted, but then the helicopter flew away and they remained in the open, staring up at the sky, praying that this would not turn out to be a false alarm and that it would return.

At 10.20 Neill heard the sound of a helicopter again, but only a glimpse could be seen and they all wondered why the aircraft was flying so high.

Another night followed, and Neill noticed that his urine had changed from dark yellow to a much more disturbing yellow-brown. He knew he had to take in more water or his kidneys might be damaged. The other all-pervading factor was the vile smell of rotting boots and decaying clothes. However many times they washed them with soap, the garments retained the awful stench of decomposition.

Indeed, it was rather as if the gully was slowly eating the expedition alive.

On this occasion, at the very last minute, however, it was cheated of its prey. On Friday, 25 March, the thirtieth day of the expedition, an Alouette helicopter flew up the gully, so near to the rock walls that Neill thought the aircraft was going to crash.

As it hovered right over him, Foster indicated FIVE with one hand and showed two fingers and held his stomach with the other. A yellow bag on a thin nylon cord was lowered, and when the expedition ripped it open they discovered, to their surprise, that it contained British Army rations.

Inside the bag was the most welcome note any of them had ever received:

HELP IS ON ITS WAY. ENCLOSED ARE RATIONS.

The next part of the message was obliterated because the bag had, inevitably, fallen into a pool of water. It ended, however,

HANG ON IN THERE LADS

They were saved. The survivors could hardly believe that the much hoped for, much dreamt about rescue had arrived at last.

Despite his protests, Neill was taken off first, and the weather closed in again as the gully appeared to make one last attempt to destroy its captives. But they already had food, medical supplies and radios, so it was too late.

Eventually the remaining four were lifted out, only to discover that the reconnaissance party had safely regained civilization.

The rescue had been a British Army operation in conjunction with the Malaysians – an operation on a huge scale – and Neill and Foster realized, as they recovered, that their plight had been a subject of far greater concern than they had ever believed.

CHAPTER 16

THE BOMBARDMENT

Suzy Wighton survived the siege of the Palestinian refugee camps. At the time she was a young nurse who, in September 1986, arrived as a volunteer to work in the Bourj al-Brajneh camp in the Lebanon. Her role was to work in the camp clinic, looking after the everyday needs of the refugees as well as any minor injuries they might receive.

Within days of her arrival, Suzy was faced with a blood-bath when the camp came under bombardment from the Amal Shi'ite Muslim Militia, which was one of Lebanon's many warring factions. They set about the indiscriminate killing and wounding of men, women and children as well as the destruction of their homes and property. The Amal also calculatingly blocked essential supplies getting into the camp.

There were many appeals for help from the West from a number of different refugee camps in the area, and the following is a typical appeal from the Beirut refugee camp of Shatila.

'The rockets and artillery and all the weapons which pounded our camp for four months and which destroyed 950 of its houses, have fallen silent. However, for nine long months conditions have been as unbearable and inhuman as any suffered since the dawn of history.

'Despite our protestations we live without

electricity or fresh water. The rubbish piles up and the sewage flows everywhere. It being summer now, many are sick, suffering vomiting, typhoid, and skin diseases. The schools are destroyed and their pupils forbidden to leave the camp to study, as are the sick who are thus denied the aid of medical specialists.

'Winter approaches. 950 houses lie in ruins with the remainder unfit for human habitation. Yet building materials are not allowed into the camp whilst 1,000 people languish without shelter. A social disaster is impending."

Ironically, however, it was the last-ditch appeal from Suzy Wighton, Pauline Cutting and a Dutch nurse, Ben Alofs, which produced the media coverage of the plight of the refugees and the terrible state of their camps that shocked the rest of the world and eventually prompted the lifting of the siege.

Suzy's diary is not just filled with her own entries, it also includes entries from many refugees who regularly came to the medical centre to tell her their feelings and experiences.

The conditions reflected in these diaries are appalling. Thousands of refugees were reduced to eating pets and living in bunkers below open sewers. Even so, hundreds died from sniping, and the shelling and rocket attacks which had already reduced their homes to rubble. Suzy's diaries have been described as a people's witness and are a testament to those who died as well as those who survived.

Originally, the Bourj al-Brajneh camp held 16,000 people, mostly families, but when the camp came under siege as a result of what was known as the Six Month War, so many refugees managed to escape that the population fell to 8,500.

The first day of the war came on 29 October, 1986, but the following day was quiet after a peaceful night. They woke, ate breakfast, and gathered more emergency equipment. Suzy Wighton made gauze and attempted to sterilize it, but there was no electricity. Hospital personnel were anxious about Pauline, Ben, Hannes and Suzy going out of the camp to the meeting in Hamra, so they decided to return at 16.00 at the latest. The meeting was a hurried one, and the group returned to the camp in two ambulances in the early afternoon.

Suzy initially returned to a domestic disaster. Hussein, one of the refugees, had drowned a small kitten that she had become very fond of. She was extremely angry and very upset, as he had been warned not to touch it.

Later she heard a whoosh accompanied by a flare, and was told it was a B-7 rocket. Suddenly all hell broke loose in the camp, with crowds running about in the street, trying to find protection. The war had finally come.

Suzy and her colleagues ran to carry all the equipment downstairs to set up an emergency room. This was an extremely dangerous operation as the camp was surrounded by snipers, but they managed to bring most of the stuff down, crouching and crawling up the stairs. The fighting had started with one of Sultan Abu Riyad's bodyguards being shot; Ben and Pauline had tried to resuscitate him, but had failed. Meanwhile, the defensive positions around the camp were carefully inspected, and it was noticed that the Syrian post was very well sandbagged. They settled in, knowing the camp could be under siege for some time. Ironically, many refugees seemed to fail to realize the hopelessness of their position, or perhaps the drama had gone to their heads. Friends took photos of each other holding rifles.

Suzy went to the hospital to fetch supplies because another refugee had burnt his arm on his gun. As she went, she realized that many of those in the camp were going to harm themselves with their weapons, perhaps almost as many as would be shot by snipers. She also realized that she must save water in case the electricity remained erratic and the pump wouldn't work.

As the days passed, the carnage was increasing. Typically, Suzy's nursing was continuously interrupted. One of the injured was carried into the clinic by his grandmother, quickly followed by another relative who was bleeding from multiple shrapnel wounds. Another problem arose out of the female relatives' concern for the maintenance of modesty while Suzy was trying to clean the wounds of an injured woman. She wanted to get it done as quickly as possible, but on lifting the woman's dress her attentions were firmly resisted by the relatives, and every attempt to apply a quick dressing was disrupted. Eventually Suzy prevailed, but the process took a long time and the victim became increasingly cold and shocked.

'One of the stretcher bearers from this morning is dead, shot in the chest four times with an M-16. He was rushed past here to the hospital, face down and bleeding from the chest, although some said he was already dead. They didn't position him correctly or bring him here for resuscitation or haemorrhage pads. Everyone shocked and shouting.'

Three more refugees died that day, from either rocket attacks or sniper fire. A Lebanese Army 240mm shell hit a house, destroyed a room and severely injured a young mother. An old man under treatment died of heart failure in the night before he could be taken to the hospital, and now a younger man had also been killed.

They were all so young, thought Suzy, so terribly young. An orthopaedic surgeon refused to come into the camp because he was afraid he would die there. Suzy and her medical colleagues knew the feeling but they had no thought of leaving, despite the fact that the deadly Lebanese shells were being increasingly used against them. She was now sure they were determined to kill every refugee in the camp. The radio had said the Amal had stopped shooting, but there was no indication of that as people passed the clinic, guns clanking against belts and bullet pouches.

The conditions that Suzy and her colleagues were working in continued to deteriorate and the danger to their lives increased, but she barely gave the situation a thought, always presenting an ironic sense of humour and maintaining a tight focus on the continually increasing number of patients.

Christmas Day (Day 58 of the siege) was routine hell, and Suzy woke knowing that her already inadequate medical supplies were fast diminishing. Rockets flew early in the morning, and then the wounded began banging on the clinic door, letting themselves in and demanding dressings, even though the notice on the door said, 'Closed for dressings. Only emergencies today.' But then everyone thought they were an emergency. Later that night, when Suzy was trying to sleep, two refugees, Akram and Shehadi al Ashwa, let themselves in and shook her awake to deal with a boy with a burn.

She went out to provide essential dressings and was immediately waylaid by a number of people. Wafiqa al Ashwa, looking wan and ill, took her in for coffee for Christmas. Although she was a Muslim she was celebrating Maryam (Mary) and Isa (Jesus, a prophet in Islam). She asked Suzy if she knew some way of taking her son Akram out of the country to be educated, as the wars were putting an end to all school lessons, in and out of the camp. Suzy told her she would ask Pauline (Cutting) to see how possible this was when she returned to London.

Suzy then visited Ahmad, another of the injured, dressing his wounds. Someone was making bread, so after Wafiqa's biscuits for Christmas she also got fresh hot bread. She was not to relax for long, however, as two injured men arrived, the first with mild shrapnel wounds, the second, Yusuf, with respiratory arrest. At first Suzy found his pulse beating weakly, but as he appeared not to be breathing she put an airway suction device down his throat and blew hard. His lungs inflated and he started coughing, so she suctioned and took out the airway. Almost immediately he stopped breathing again, so she put the airway back in, blew again and suctioned until he was coughing and semi-conscious. With her colleagues, she took him up to the clinic, prodding his chest every so often. They got there and he recovered. Once again, Suzy had found the strength to bring someone back from the dead. She decided against returning to her room, however, as the rockets and shells shrieked over the camp, all too often finding their human targets.

On Day 86, Suzy recorded that conditions had reached a new low.

'Food is running out and now all we can talk about is when we will have to eat the cats and rats (the latter are not such a good idea as they are very dirty). The hospital does represent an experiment in sensory deprivation, as Pauline commented yesterday, no light, water everywhere, no noise except when working, and nowhere to go. To walk through it is like walking through Kafka's The Trial, *as filmed by Orson Welles. Dark imperceptible shadowy humans standing in whispering corners, against whispering walls, impossible to see unless they brush against you; wet underfoot, darkness, relying only on memory to guide you through the labyrinth. Sat having a dismally ironic conversation with Hisham (broth-*

er of Salah the radiographer) about food, more food, the hostages, [several westerners werebeing held in Beirut] the war and the deteriorating situation over the past year in the Lebanon. Then we sat in the alternating dark and light, as the generator went on and off, dreaming of all kinds of food, from cheeseburgers, chips, salads and coffee to cigarettes, chicken, roast beef, Yorkshire pudding, potatoes, horseradish sauce, etc., a bottle of whisky, coffee and more cigarettes.'

Between them, Pauline Cutting, Ben Alofs and Suzy issued a statement to the world's media. They signed the statement which was issued via walkie-talkie through Dr Mohamad Ossman in Akka Hospital. It read:

DECLARATION FROM FOREIGN HEALTH WORKERS IN
BOURJ AL-BRAJNEH REFUGEE CAMP

We, as foreign health workers, living and working in Bourj al-Brajneh refugee camp, declare that the situation in the camp is critical and conditions inhumane. The camp has now been under siege for more than twelve weeks and the 8,500 residents are being subjected to conditions of deprivation and misery. Drinking water is the most basic human need. Most houses do not have running drinking water and it has to be collected daily from taps in the street at great risk of personal safety. Several women have been shot and killed collecting water for their families. Food stocks have been completely depleted. There is now no baby food or milk and babies are drinking tea and water. There is no flour and therefore no bread, no fresh food, so pregnant women and children are suffering undernourishment. People are eating stale food and suffering vomiting and diarrhoea. Many families now have no food. It is winter and the electricity was cut off from the camp two and a half months ago. People are cold and have chest infections. There are huge piles of garbage which cannot be cleared and rats are thriving. One old lady who was bedridden was unable to get help when her foot was eaten by rats for three

*consecutive nights before she was rescued. The
constant bombardment of the camp forces the people to crowd into poorly ventilated shelters with
no sanitation or to risk being blown up at home.
Hundreds of children have scabies and many
have severe skin infections. Approximately 35 per
cent of homes in Bourj al-Brajneh have now been
destroyed. In the hospital, many medicines have
run out and we have no more gauze. The hospital
building is being rendered unstable by repeated
shelling and patients and nurses have been
injured by shrapnel. Water is dripping down the
walls and mould is growing in every room.*

*We declare these conditions to be inhumane and
on humanitarian grounds we call for the lifting of
the siege and the admission of food and medicines
by the international relief agencies.*

> *DR PAULINE CUTTING – British Surgeon*
> *BEN ALOFS – Dutch Nurse*
> *SUSAN WIGHTON – Scottish Nurse*

Eventually, after continuous delays and much
obstruction by the Amal, the siege was lifted and
supplies, as well as horrified members of the
press, were let in.

Suzy Wighton left the camp but returned to
witness its final stand and eventual destruction
in July 1988 by the rival Abu Musa group who

were backed by the Syrians.

Her last glimpse was appalling as a mass grave was being filled.

She was stopped on the way by a BBC camera team, but avoided them, telling them that her friends were being buried. Women screamed and fainted as the bloated bodies were tipped off stretchers into the large grave.

'We cried, sitting in the shade, with the spades and stretchers left around us in the sand; the new earth mounds bare except for the palm fronds of a recent burial. Another blue-skied day, another day of tears.'

It is inconceivable that all four engines of a Boeing 747 would fail for apparently no reason. Yet this happened to BA Flight 009 on 24 June 1982 under the command of Captain Eric Moody, on its way from Kuala Lumpur to Australia.

As the British Airways aircraft flew over Java the night sky was suddenly illuminated by unearthly displays of St Elmo's fire. Then smoke filled the cabin of the Boeing and flames appeared to surround the plane as it was tossed about by extensive turbulence. Eventually, one after the other, and for no reason the crew could immediately explain, the engines surged and failed.

This left the Boeing powerless, with additional damage and no forward vision. As Captain Moody tried desperately to control the crippled aircraft, his co-pilot sent out the Mayday calls and the engineer struggled to restart the stricken engines.

Because the public address system had also mysteriously broken down, the cabin crew had to try and calm the 247 passengers as the Boeing dropped towards the mountains below.

Betty Tootell was one of the passengers on BA 009, and as she already had a civil aviation background she was able to use her knowledge discerningly. She and her mother, Phyl Welch, had decided to read Jane Austen throughout the long flight. Betty read *Mansfield Park* and Phyl read *Northanger Abbey*. They were sitting in Row 55 and had effectively shut out the plastic modern world around them. The aircraft was cruising steadily at 37,000 feet, the cabin crew had just served the passengers a light meal and the blinds were being pulled down in readiness for the film, *On Golden Pond*. No one was to see it.

Betty glanced up from her book when slight turbulence shook the aircraft. She looked out of the window and was surprised to see '*a flickering, brilliant silver-white light*'. She watched it for a little while, believing the sight to be a miniature form of Aurora Borealis (northern lights), which she had once seen on the polar route. Yet the effect was clinging to the aircraft, flickering along and around that part of the port wing which was visible from where she was sitting. Maybe it wasn't the Aurora Borealis, she thought. It was more like the shimmering effect which she had occasionally noticed hovering around the wings of aircraft in broad daylight, especially on bright sunny days, almost like a heat haze. Now it was dark outside, and the shimmering was vividly bright.

Betty tried to convince herself that the effect was nothing abnormal, particularly as none of the other passengers seemed to have noticed it. She attempted to carry on with her book, but found that she was reading the same sentence again and again without taking in a single word.

Her mother, who had a slightly different angle of vision, was watching a turquoise-and-pink tinted cloud which gradually seemed to be getting pinker. She had seen similar colours before in a beautiful sunset, but this seemed rather ominous.

The American-built Boeing 747 was the first giant wide-bodied, high-capacity jet airliner, and the largest aeroplane ever build for commercial purposes. The plane was divided into five passenger cabins, A to E, running fore to aft, with another cabin out of sight at the upper level behind the flight deck. The Boeing's tail height was equivalent to a six-storey building. Six and a half metres wide, it had a wing span of almost sixty metres, a length of nearly seventy-one metres and a weight of over 350 tonnes. When the aircraft was fully pressurised, another tonne of air was added to its weight.

Boeing had been deeply concerned about safety, and their Boeing 747 test programme – laboratory, flight and static tests – was the most extensive ever undertaken. The fatigue-test programme took the airframe through the equivalent of 20,000 airline flights, or 60,000 hours. Then, hundreds of additional checks were made, including one that placed the equivalent of 12,000 further

flying hours on a damaged structure, to make
sure the aircraft would continue to operate safely
even in extreme conditions.

The Boeing 747 cabin could accommodate 452
mixed-class passengers. British Airways, however, wanting to increase comfort, had spaced the
seats more widely so that, even if all the seats
were occupied, the plane carried just under 400
passengers. The passenger list had been far short
of that on this particular flight.

Stewardess Fiona Wright was in the upstairs
first-class passenger cabin where there were no
passengers. She had just finished a rest day in
Kuala Lumpur and had spent all her currency
and had no cash for a meal before boarding the
aircraft. As there were only a few passengers on
the lower deck, she had decided to take an early
meal herself. She had just started eating when
Senior First Officer Greaves telephoned her, sug-
gesting she come up to the flight deck. *You won't
believe your eyes,'* he told her.

When she arrived, the deck was in semi-
darkness (normal for night flying) and Fiona was
amazed to see what looked like a silver-white
firework display, things like sparkler or even
welding sparks hitting the windscreen. As they
made impact, the sparks seemed to become
brighter.

SFO Greaves told her to fetch the Captain

quickly, and she hurried away to find him.

Meanwhile, back in the cabin, the passengers were beginning to notice a thickening smoke haze. It was dark and many had switched on their reading lights.

A search began for a smouldering cigarette but nothing came to light. Meanwhile, the haze continued to thicken, and the flight crew gazed at the strange effects on the windscreen – as if millions of machine-gun tracer bullets or sparks were being hurled at it. The only comparison they could make was to St Elmo's fire – a luminosity or even a ball of light occasionally seen on aircraft and ships during a storm, and usually associated with cirrus or electrically charged cloud. This often takes the form of forks of lightning running up the windscreen, but the effect they were now seeing was rather different.

By now the passengers had become alarmed by the strange phenomena and so had the crew. Cabin Service Officer Skinner was watching the visual effects carefully. They were rather like flashes of forked lightning, short, zig-zagging, with splashes of emerald green that seemed to come right through the window. In the background was a bright, shining, sparkling effect which reminded him of car headlights in a heavy rainstorm.

SFO Greaves was looking backwards out of the window on his right-hand side and glancing towards the front of the No 4 engine. He was amazed by what he saw. The engine was lit up as if there was a searchlight inside.

When Captain Moody returned to the flight deck, he also saw the weird effect of the brilliant magnesium-white brightness lighting the engine from behind the fan. He could see the fan turning, and the stroboscopic effect made the fan blades appear to be going backwards.

Senior Engineering Officer Barry Townley-Freeman was also watching. It was most alarming and he noted that every detail of the intake fan and spinner was visible, lit up from inside, glowing incandescent, like sparks from a grinding wheel.

From the flight deck CSO Skinner saw a magnesium-white light on the leading edge of the wings and engines and inside the engine nacelles. He headed downstairs, ready to prepare for an emergency by clearing the cabin and galleys so that any loose objects could not become lethal flying weapons.

As Stewardess Wright moved back into the upper-deck passenger cabin she could detect a musty sort of smell as if something had fused. She decided to return to the flight deck and tell the crew, but then had another idea. Quickly, she switched off the upper-galley electrical equipment, the boilers, the ovens and refrigerators, and safely stowed and secured equipment.

As she went down the staircase to the passenger cabin, Purser Abrey arrived to report to the CSO the presence of smoke in the rear cabin.

By this time the smoke haze was very marked, accompanied by the ionized smell associated with electrical problems.

SEO Townley-Freeman was watching the instruments for any sign of trouble. He had smelt the smoke and had quickly re-checked for any sign of fire, but all seemed normal. He also knew that smoke could occur as a result of air-conditioning or electrical troubles without there being any fire. The smell suggested the latter.

Alarm spread amongst the passengers, who now suspected the engines were on fire, and Betty heard the 'ping' as the *Fasten Seat Belts* sign was illuminated. Once again she tried to read, but couldn't concentrate.

A flashing white light that had appeared to be lightning had now spread along the entire length of the starboard wing. Smoke was coming out of the vents in the wing and a continuous sheet of flame passed just below the windows of the aircraft.

So far there had been no announcements on the tannoy and the cabin crew, united and calm, went around the passengers, reassuring them, telling them a variety of hurriedly invented reasons for the strange effects.

'It's just friction,' explained one of the stewards, hoping he sounded convincing.

'Don't walk fast – walk slowly,' another steward was advised by a senior colleague. No one knew what was happening – not even the flight crew – and it was essential to avoid panic.

One passenger, Maurice Castel, then noticed what appeared to be thick dust in the cabin and was certain that the pressurization system had failed and that this had caused dust to rise from the fabric and fittings.

Then came an explosion from the engine on his

right, and Castel saw some passengers pull down their window blinds. Out of sight, out of mind, seemed to be the reaction, particularly as the cabin crew had been so casually reassuring. It was fortunate the passengers did not realize the extent of the problem. But at this stage neither did anyone else.

Not all the passengers were reassured, and some became certain that the aircraft was on fire and would shortly plunge into the sea. There was still no panic, however, and an atmosphere of brooding calm seemed to fill the cabin.

At 13.42 GMT No 4 engine failed. Initially this did not present a major problem and Captain Moody flew the Boeing on the remaining three engines while his colleagues carried out fire drills.

Then at 13.43 GMT No 2 engine surged and died. This was serious, but it would still be possible to fly the aircraft and land safely on two engines.

Unbelievably, however, before the fire drill could be started for No 2 engine, the remaining No 1 and No 3 engines surged – and then simultaneously shut down. BA Flight 009 was gliding.

As far as the flight-deck crew were aware, incidents of multiple engine failure were usually the result of human error. This could either be a mistake about the fuel supply or failure to operate the de-icing system in freezing conditions. But these systems had already been checked as well as the igniters and circuit-breakers. All were in order. At approximately 13.44 GMT Captain Moody told SFO Greaves to declare an emergency. He also ordered the four-engine failure drill while continuing to fly the aircraft totally without engine power. Fortunately, he had practised a four-engine failure in the airline's Boeing 747 simulator.

Greaves made urgent contact with Jakarta Air Control Centre. Using the airline's call sign and flight number he called: *'Mayday, Mayday. Speedbird Nine. We have lost all four engines. Out of 370 [37,000 feet].'*

Fatuously, Jakarta ACC then replied, *'Speedbird Nine, have you got a problem?'*

Trying to control his frustration, the First Officer tried again, *'Jakarta Control. Speedbird Nine. We have lost all four engines. Now out of 360.'*

Jakarta appeared to misunderstand yet again, and replied, *'Speedbird Nine. You have lost number four engine?'*

Grimly, Greaves tried again. *'Jakarta Control. Speedbird Nine has lost* ALL FOUR ENGINES, *repeat* ALL FOUR ENGINES. *Now descending through flight level 350.'*

This time Jakarta ACC seemed completely unable to hear what he was saying.

However, Garuda Indonesian Airways Flight GA 875, which was in the vicinity, *did* hear the exchange and intervened. *'Jakarta. Garuda 875.'*

'Go ahead,' acknowledged Jakarta ACC.

Garuda Flight 875 quickly repeated the first message, *'Speedbird Nine has lost four engines, lost four engines, out of 370.'*

Jakarta now seemed to understand, and acknowledged the message. The time was approximately 13.45 GMT.

Meanwhile, with no hard information from the tannoy system as yet, the passengers were alarmed but still remained superficially calm.

SEO Townley-Freeman started the 'loss-of-all-generators' drill, assuming that the loss of all engines meant the loss of all generators. This drill consisted of checking that the battery was on – as it should always be – and ensuring that the electrical stand-by was powered. Supplies could be taken from it for trying to re-start engines, flying the aircraft, and for one radio.

Townley-Freeman switched off the fuel to re-schedule the control unit for re-starting, checked that the aircraft was in the correct height/speed band, switched on the igniters and opened the fuel valves again.

The engines should then have re-started. But they didn't.

Complete mystification followed while Captain Moody racked his brains desperately. He knew that at the start of the emergency the aircraft was flying at a height of 37,000 feet. But now the Boeing had lost all of its own sources of motive power. As one of the rather obvious principles of flying, an aircraft needs sufficient forward speed to prevent it from stalling and plunging downwards. but for the moment Captain Moody could try to convert height into forward speed by dropping the nose of the aircraft, which would, in turn, provide enough lift to keep the aircraft gliding. He thought he might be able to control the Boeing's descent in a controlled glide at an equally controlled rate. All this would depend upon the speed which he required and upon the aerodynamic qualities of the Boeing 747. It was a considerable gamble.

The descent from the aircraft's original position of 37,000 feet to sea level would take about twenty-three minutes and would cover a ground distance of 141 nautical miles, resulting in an average glide slope of 3 degrees.

These figures, however, were based upon a gross weight of 500,000 pounds and assumed an idle thrust setting on the engines, pre-supposing a 'clean' condition, i.e. with flaps and landing gear retracted. They were also based upon an ideal, non-emergency situation which couldn't be further from the present circumstances.

Slowly, the passengers became aware that the aircraft was descending. Still calm prevailed. The Purser imagined they were experiencing some kind of engine trouble because of the flames and the smoke, but he relied on the highly experienced flight crew – and the passengers relied on the equally experienced cabin attendants. Somehow this equation had to be maintained, despite the many anxious questions beginning to be asked, questions that still had to be delicately parried. As for the lack of engine noise, the Purser imagined that an engine had been feathered to quieten it down, or that the aircraft had reduced speed. He had known the situation to have occurred before; it had always been corrected and the plane had continued on its flight quite normally.

Nevertheless, the cabin crew went into instant emergency action, taking care to continue to act as calmly and casually as possible.

By now of course they all knew the Boeing was involved in some inexplicable emergency. As a result, they hurriedly placed glasses, tea and coffee pots, cups and saucers and trays into the refrigerators and cupboards. They quickly cleared the galleys, stowed all loose items, secured and locked the galley doors, and switched off the electrical supplies throughout the aircraft. They double- and triple-checked to make sure that this was accomplished. The cabin crew then made sure that the passengers' seat belts were fastened, their tables stowed, and the last remaining odd cups and glasses were removed.

They checked that the exit doors were completely free from obstruction, and moved or secured any loose items of baggage or personal possessions so that any emergency passenger movement would not be impeded. This procedure had been rehearsed so many times in their training sessions that their actions were virtually automatic.

On the flight deck desperate attempts were being made to re-start the engines. The Boeing was still above the recommended altitude of 28,000 feet below which engine re-starts are considered more likely to succeed, but this was rather different. The aircraft had a four-engine failure and there could be no question of waiting for the recommended height.

Yet the engines were still windmilling and, as a result, still producing a reasonable quantity of hydraulic and electrical power. Also, the rotation of the turbines was sufficient for the pumps to deliver full hydraulic power for the flying controls.

The safe land clearance height in the area over which the aircraft had passed before crossing the coast was 11,500 feet. Java has high mountain ranges, and Captain Moody decided to keep the aircraft heading south across the Indian Ocean, away from the land. The automatic pilot was still engaged.

At 13.46 GMT SFO Greaves had again made contact with Jakarta, this time requesting radar assistance, but although Jakarta acknowledged the appeal they couldn't see the Boeing on their radar and could therefore offer no help.

At about 30,000 feet, with the engine re-starts still unsuccessful, Captain Moody decided to set the aircraft in a gentle left-hand turn back towards the north and Java. SFO Greaves kept Jakarta informed.

The aircraft began its turn. At about 13.47 GMT Jakarta called, *"Speedbird Nine. Radar cannot see you. Squawk Alpha 7700."* (A request to the aircraft to transmit the emergency transponder code.)

Hurriedly SFO Greaves replied, *"Jakarta. Speedbird Nine. We are already squawking 7700."* Then he wondered if the poor communications with Jakarta could be due to the mysterious influence the Boeing was under.

Not only were the transmissions weak, but there was also considerable interference on the VHF radios, something which was virtually unknown except in the vicinity of electrical storms. Usually an intermittent crackling would be heard, rather like the interference on a domestic radio or television set, but this was different – a noisy static was now assaulting the headsets of the three flight deck crew. There was no explanation. It was rather as if the Boeing had been bewitched.

Meanwhile, the First Officer and Flight Engineer were going through the engine re-start drill yet again, but still nothing happened and the Boeing was going down at 2,000 feet per minute. They were bewildered and the fear was pounding in them. Fortunately, so was the adrenalin.

A jet engine operates in a continuous cycle, with air coming in at the front, passing through compressors, mixing with fuel and then, once ignited, burning in the combustion chambers. It expands through the turbines producing the power, a small amount of which is diverted to drive the compressors. Under normal conditions the engine's igniters are off and are switched on only when starting or re-starting.

In this emergency, as long as the air was entering at the correct rate of flow, the compressors were turning, the fuel was flowing and the igniters were switched on with the circuit-breakers in, the engines should have re-started and continued to burn.

Captain Moody knew that it was essential to keep the indicated airspeed of the aircraft in the critical 250-270-knot range to assist the engines to reignite, but SFO Greaves noticed that the airspeed indicator on his side was showing 320 knots, and when he brought this to the attention of the Captain he replied that the indicator on his side showed 270 knots.

The 50-knot difference was inexplicable and added to the mystery that was rapidly becoming a disaster.

Still the engines wouldn't fire, and Captain Moody wondered whether the airspeed-indicator discrepancy could be at the heart of the problem.

Because he could no longer be certain about the navigation system readouts, he decided to fly the Boeing at varying speeds extending below and above the 250-270 knot range in the hope that at some stage he would get the correct impetus at which the engines might re-start.

The lack of engine noise as the Boeing kept going down increased the number of questions from the passengers.

Stewardess Susan Glennie had a quick answer

for all of them. *'Put it this way. When you see the flight crew followed by the cabin crew heading towards the rear of the aircraft carrying parachutes, then you know we've got problems. Until then, there's absolutely nothing to worry about.'* The loss of power was now starting to have an effect on the aircraft pressurization, which operates by allowing more air into the aircraft than is allowed to leak out. The air is first heated and then passes into the cabin. It leaks out through the outflow valves at a controlled rate sufficient to maintain the cabin pressure at that of an altitude of about 6,500 feet, even when the aircraft is at 37,000 feet. The flow rate varies with the altitude and the atmosphere; the less dense the atmosphere, the less the oxygen.

Now, however, although the outflow valves had closed to try to compensate, the loss of engine power had reduced the normal inward airflow and the normal cabin pressure could no longer be maintained and had started to fall.

The aircraft had by now descended to 26,000 feet. On the flight deck, the pressure warning sounded, indicating that the cabin pressure had fallen to the equivalent of 10,000 feet.

The flight-deck crew immediately put on their oxygen masks and steeled themselves for the inevitable. It was now going to be necessary to alert the passengers to some little problems.

Purser Sarah de Lane Lea reached the control box for the public address system first. She pressed the manual back-up button which would correct any automatic failure and operated the pre-recorded oxygen mask briefing. But that, too, failed to operate.

Next a 'live' announcement was tried over the public address system by pressing the square override button on the wall panel and using the passenger address microphone, but this, like the engines, didn't work either and panic surged through the cabin crew's minds. Nothing was going to work – and everyone was going to die.

Araf Chohan was standing next to Fiona Wright. He asked her quietly, *'Are you afraid?... I'm afraid... Do you think we'll pull through?'*

'Don't worry about things like that,' she replied quickly. *'We're all right.'*

The attempted reassurances sounded very hollow.

CSO Skinner also turned to Fiona Wright. *'Do you remember me telling you about my headache yesterday?'* he said, attempting to lighten the atmosphere. *'Well, I think it's coming back!'*

They knew there was only one crude method of communicating with the passengers left – the megaphones, which were placed throughout the aircraft for simultaneous use by members of the cabin crew. Using them, they eventually reas-

sured the passengers about the appearance of
their oxygen masks, which had produced a new
threat.

When the masks dropped, Janet Miller didn't
know how to apply one to her baby son, David,
who was only four months old. She asked for help
from a stewardess who remained with her,
helping with oxygen for the baby and once again
trying to reassure Janet that everything would
be all right. In fact, the stewardess sounded so
convincing that she reassured all those in the
near vicinity, but as far as Janet herself was
concerned, she was privately certain the engines
were on fire and that the Boeing was going to
crash.At this stage, the aircraft's height was
down to 16,000 feet and Captain Moody knew
that he was not going to be able to reach
Jakarta's Halim Airport to attempt an unpow-
ered landing. It was too distant and there were
mountains in the way. Worse still, a successful
crash landing in this sort of terrain in pitch darkness was going to be impossible.

As the safe land-clearance height was 11,500
feet, the Captain decided that if the engines had
not re-started before 12,000 feet, he would turn
south again, away from the mountains and head
out to sea in a move that would only gain him an
extra five or six minutes at most to try and get
the so mysteriously silenced engines to start up

again. If they wouldn't, then he had already decided to ditch the Boeing in the sea.

The ditching of a Boeing 747 had never been attempted before, but Captain Moody knew that the engines would sheer off on impact. The engine mounts were designed with a structural fuse – a purpose-designed part of the structure – which would fail before the wings could be affected. This meant the engine struts and engines would break away without harming vital wing fuel tanks and other structures.

A successful ditching also depended not only on wind direction but also on primary and secondary ocean swells. Nevertheless, this was beginning to look like his only choice.

Betty Tootell noticed that *'the cabin lights went right out again, but for longer this time. With only the EXIT signs shining brilliantly against the blackness it seemed the clearest possible way of telling us to be ready to get out and to know, even in the darkness, where our nearest escape exit was located...'*

"I must take my handbag – my passport is in it," said my mother, but immediately realized the futility of it all, and, despite everything, we both smiled.'

Betty, sitting at the rear of the aircraft, wondered if the tail would break off on impact, and she and her mother would be thrown clear. *'The thought was totally selfish, and even as it crossed my mind I had the grace to feel ashamed, but the will to live is compellingly strong. I tested the distance to the seat in front of me to find out if my head would strike it on impact, and decided which bracing position we should adopt when it became necessary.'*

She put her arms around her mother's shoulders and together they linked the fingers of their free hands as tightly as they could in the hope that they would not be torn apart in the crash and thereby suffer the misery of losing each other.

Betty afterwards summed up her feelings as follows:

'Fear? Yes, of course. Anger? Resentment? Frustration? Yes, but not as great as the overwhelmingly intense feeling of just not wanting to die. A feeling of total aversion to death. All the things not accomplished, not finished.'

As Betty thought her terrible thoughts Captain Moody headed the aircraft out over the sea, checking the time they had been without motive power. It was just over 12 minutes and the Boeing had descended almost 24,000 feet. The restarting process continued, but still the engines refused to fire. Then, without the slightest warning, No 4 engine roared. The first to fail was now alive again. Greaves radioed Jakarta, but was still unsure whether ground control was picking up his message. Eighty-two seconds later, No 3 engine also refired and Captain Moody was able to gain height. What was more, the radio transmissions between Jakarta and the Boeing were suddenly fully restored.

The crew's hopes soared, particularly as the aircraft could not only fly but also land on two engines. Seconds later, engines 1 and 2 restarted, and Jakarta had Speedbird Nine back on radar. Captain Moody spoke to the passengers on the mysteriously restored intercom: *'Ladies and gentlemen. This is the Captain speaking. We seem to have overcome the problems and have managed to start all the engines. We are diverting to Jakarta and expect to land in about fifteen minutes.'*

To the passengers these simple words of confirmation about the engines conveyed the wonderful realization that everything was going to be 'all right', but on the flight deck, as the Boeing climbed to 15,000 feet, the St Elmo's fire returned and No 2 engine began to surge again. Hurriedly, the crew shut it down and Captain Moody throttled back to reduce power.

As the Boeing descended towards Jakarta airport, the airspeed indicators began to read the same again. What was the strange power of the heights that had attacked them so mysteriously and brutally?

The aircraft made a smooth landing and spontaneous applause and cheering broke out amongst the passengers. People embraced, champagne was opened.

As Captain Moody went downstairs, he saw layers of gritty black dust on every surface. When he returned to the flight deck, and commented on the phenomenon, SEO Townley-Freeman, who had been in Jakarta a few weeks before, suddenly remembered an item he had seen in a local newspaper.

'It's volcanic ash,' he said, and he was right. Mount Galunggung had erupted after a long period of relative quiet, erupted with greater force than ever before. The wind had been blowing in a south-westerly direction and the dense ash and dust cloud spread a thick mass of debris high into the sky.

BA 009 had been approaching from the north and Captain Moody had been totally unaware of the danger. The dust had choked the engines, and when the Boeing was inspected at the airport the damage was incredible, with a shot-blasted effect all over its body.

Reflecting on the appalling experience, Captain Moody felt sure that having flown through the debris of the eruption, the aircraft had eventually emerged into clean air allowing the engines to re-start. When they tried to climb again they re-encountered the ash and the engines began to fail.

Betty later remembered: *'Few of us will ever forget our experience that night. Does it seem strange that many of us never* want *to? And that from the safe vantage point of survival we would not have missed it for anything?*

'Perhaps, if you were not there, this all sounds trite and over-emotional. But the impression was very vivid and powerful, and I believe that there was some sort of message there for all of us. A message that will be personal and as different for each one of us as we are different from one another'

CHAPTER 18
PONGO DE MAINIQUE

O f all the great travel writers Peter Matthiessen is one of the most adventurous, and one of the greatest tests of his nerve must have been his 1960 expedition by raft down the Pongo in Peru, a river ominously known as the Black Drunken River by the local Indians who accompanied him.

The *balsa*, or raft, that they used had been constructed by the local Indians according to traditional methods, using logs that were already cut and dried as well as some green poles. More of the latter were brought by two Indians who arrived in a canoe, clinging to the slippery poles that had been gathered upriver. Matthiessen writes, *'They were soon notched and spiked and lashed together, and it occurs to me with rather a start that we are actually on the brink of risking our lives.'*

His dread grew even greater when he was told about the twenty-foot waves on the river. One of the Indians had put forward the theory that the passage of the Pongo in the rainy season is less dangerous than in the dry season, because the most dangerous rocks are covered over. Matthiessen sincerely hoped he was right.

'Whatever the truth of the matter, we are casting off at midday. I'm not at all sure we know all we should, and would feel much happier with a life preserver. I asked Epitanio if he thought we would make it to the mission at Timpia before nightfall. He and Ardiles grinned at each other in a way I disliked very much, and Pereira said, "Maybe, if you go directly." This sounded pretty sinister to me.'

Filled with considerable foreboding, Matthiessen christened the raft *Happy Days*. She consisted of four large balsawood poles, with two much smaller ones along each side, and a cargo frame mounted inside. She looked a flimsy craft and Matthiessen suggested that at least twelve more poles would make her much safer, but he was told that manoeuvrability was the objective – another alarming factor. The craft was about 18 feet long and 1½ wide. Once on board, Matthiessen, with his companion Andres, found it surprisingly stable.

The crew were three young Machiguengas and they had brought bows and arrows. They didn't speak Spanish but the fourth crew member, Alejandro, a Quechua, seemed to be able to understand what they were saying. They had been given Christian names, Toribio, Raul and Agostino.

The balsa had not gone far downriver when they drew into the bank and the three Machiguengas Indians disembarked, disappearing into the wilderness. Stupefied, Matthiessen, Andres and Alejandro sat on the balsa, wondering if they were to be the victims of an attack or desertion. A balsa can't be poled upstream and the hike back would be difficult. Most of their supplies had already gone, and all they had left were two cans of peaches, a bottle of *pisco*, a local spirit, and one of Scotch. Starvation would be quick, if drunken.

But their trepidation was unfounded as the

Indians returned with lengths of strong liana (long stems of certain climbing plants, used as ropes) which they secured to the balsa's forward cross-pole and then led back to the stern. They managed to get Alejandro to understand that from now on they should use the lianas as a safety measure – and hang on to them as hard as they could. This new warning of impending danger added further alarm to Matthiessen's anticipation of what they might expect from the Black Drunken River.

The Pongo soon began to present its deadly hazards, and the balsa was almost overwhelmed when grey waves leapt up in a narrow channel and crashed down on it. Thanks to the skill of the Indians, however, they survived the deluge. The balsa also survived the rapids, although the force of the water tilted the raft at an alarming angle.

There were also 'holes-in-the-water' where just-submerged rocks lay, and rushing white waves where rocks broke the surface. Matthiessen, Andres and the crew wore only shorts and shirts, in case they had to swim for it, though Matthiessen knew they wouldn't be able to keep afloat long in such a torrent. Their only hope lay in the solidity of the raft and the instinctive skill of the Machiguengas.

The Indians spent most of their time squatting on their heels, working with precision. They would speak to each other softly 'in little whoops', like children; when alarm did get the better of them they would shout at each other to paddle harder. On certain occasions, however, they would begin an unearthly and frenzied howling, particularly when, racing along in driving rain, they dropped over a shallow ledge. Two hundred yards ahead rose the gate-like cliffs of reddish granite – the entrance to the Pongo de Mainique, the most deadly pass on the Black Drunken River.

At once, the Indians began to struggle desperately to make a landing on a small beach of black sand just under a steep bank on the left-hand side. Toribio leapt for the beach with a liana, but he disappeared from sight in the torrent and the line pulled free. His head came up in the swirling water as the current swept him down, but he caught hold of the stern as the raft swung round and tugged her into the bank. The remaining two Indians on board tied the balsa to a strong shrub and then walked downstream on the rocks, gazing ahead at the danger to come.

The original idea, when they left Pangoa, was that they would not try the pass until morning. The passage would be dangerous enough without having the darkness to contend with. Matthiessen was becoming increasingly afraid. The afternoon was dark and gloomy, cold and with sweeping rain.

Matthiessen kept asking himself what on earth had induced him to come to this sinister place, but he also knew that there could be no turning back. The raft and its crew were already trapped in an outer canyon, between the forbidding cliff and the wild torrent. Matthiessen wanted to go ahead and get the horror of it all over with. Andres was shaking with a combination of fear and cold, and Matthiessen knew exactly how he felt.

The two Indians returned, and with what seemed undue haste untied the raft. Suddenly they were back in midstream, going at an incredible speed.

The word *pongo* means a ravine or a gorge where a river bursts through the mountains. To the Machiguengas the Pongo de Mainique is known as the Place of the Bears. The legend has it that a river monster or demon in the form of a bear lives under the water, rising up to drown those who dare to take the tumultuous passage through the gorge. A previous traveller, a Mr Jolly, had written, *'The Pongo de Mainique is the worst pass on the river... The approach was a magnificent sight. Gaunt rocks rose sheer on either side, with great white waves dashing high against them... The river thunders over huge boulders in a mass of foam and spray at a speed I estimated at forty miles an hour. The fall is from fifty to sixty feet.'*

Matthiessen observes: *'My own impressions of the Pongo are less definite, owing to a certain nervous confusion.'*

With the Indians screaming, the *Happy Days* rushed towards the entrance and struck a great swirl under the giant monolith on the east side. The balsa was sucked down into a hole, spun round twice and thankfully bobbed free. The waves came at the raft from all directions and the occupants of the balsa took several of these head on.

Then, to Matthiessen's incredulity, the raft began to sweep along in fast-running but calm water. Was this a breathing space? The sheer cliffs rose several hundred feet above them, menacing the narrow passage, overgrown with rich mosses and ferns. There were caves and rocks by the water that were jet black, as was the water itself, and the pass seemed enchanted as rain and wind swept up the canyon.

Then the Machiguengas began to yell out, and instinctively Matthiessen grabbed the lianas. So did the Indians, for there was no point in paddling now as the raft slid forward to a vast waterfall and then over the top. Looking up from the bottom of a hole they could see the waves once more coming at them from all directions. To Matthiessen's surprise, however, they were nowhere near as high as had been rumoured. In fact, the waves were probably no more than eight to twelve feet, and although they washed across the raft, they had little strength. Actually they were not really waves at all but merely the upflung boil of the vast rapids.

The raft, however, still spun, tilted, went down and then miraculously up again in the turmoil of the water and, the six of them were pushed on top of each other like flailing insects.

The Indians began to paddle furiously again and Matthiessen could see why. They were now heading through calmer waters to a large whirlpool that lay on the right-hand side of the river and presented a far greater danger than the waterfall. Despite the furious paddling, the balsa was sucked closer and closer to the whirlpool until there came a dreadful gurgling sound as the bow was drawn beneath the surface.

To more cries from the Indians which, to Matthiessen, sounded ominously like death screams, and with Alejandro and Toribio trying to scramble up the slope of the desperately tilting raft, Matthiessen thought they had at last been beaten and were going to drown. In fact the balsa didn't sink, despite the fact that she was sucked towards the hole in the vortex; if the monoliths had represented the entrance to hell, then this was hell itself.

Suddenly, as if spat out, the raft made a circuit of the whirlpool and emerged, miraculously, on the opposite rim. The Indians began to paddle frantically, and their skill forced the balsa into the current of the river again.

The next set of rapids seemed nothing to the demonic power of the whirlpool.

A few minutes later, they were approaching the lower gates of the Pongo. Although smaller than the portals at the entrance to the gorge, these rocks were rectangular and the moss, ferns and lavender-coloured flowers of a vine falling down the face of the left-hand cliff, made the place seem like some mystic landscape.

Looking backwards up the canyon, Matthiessen saw the dark walls closing them off, rather as if the gates had suddenly shut. The Pongo de Mainique is the entrance to the Andes. That they had survived its deadly test was entirely due to the tenacity and instinctive skill of the Indian crew.

CHAPTER 19

SURVIVAL STORIES OF THE BLITZ

The Blitz – the intensive night bombing of London by German aircraft – began on 7 September 1940 and each night as dusk fell citizens prepared for the onslaught in a variety of different ways. Spotters on roofs waited for the first signs of the Luftwaffe as did the air-raid wardens in their control centres. All were ready to warn the public who would then seek refuge in cellars, tube stations, street shelters and crypts, whilst in the suburbs families took cover in the Anderson shelters that were sunk into in their back gardens.

Even the tube wasn't safe. Bert Woolridge, who was on duty at the ARP (Air Raid Precautions) centre in Balham, reports:

'As I went into the entrance [of Balham underground station] *hundreds of people were racing out in real panic. I got to the bottom of the stairs and the entrance to the bombed platform was blocked. All you could hear was the sound of screaming and rushing water. We managed to get to the platform by wading along through the sludge on the track, and it was terrible. People were lying there, all dead, and there was a great pile of sludge on top of them. Lots were curled up in sleeping positions on the platform. One of them – he was the porter – had had his clothes ripped off by the bomb; he lay there naked. We put the people on stretchers and carried them away*

through the water. I don't think we found any survivors that night.'

One survivor of the Blitz, George Golder, was bombed out of his dockside home in Silvertown and camped out in a brick street shelter. He remembered that he hadn't had a proper meal for days so he went home to try and find something to eat. As there was no gas or water or electricity in the house, he built a bonfire in the back garden and salvaged some bacon. He was in the middle of cooking it when the landlord came along and asked about the rent. George told him to clear off. He finished his barbecue meal but the house was in too bad a state for him to move back.

Another survivor was Emily Golder, who vividly recalled day-to-day conditions and how it was difficult to manage without being able to wash herself or her clothes, and with nowhere else to go. The council bused her family and friends out to the Majestic cinema in Woodford which was a huge, prominent building, extremely vulnerable as it was all too clearly a sitting target for the German bombers. There was nowhere to wash or eat and the survivors tried unsuccessfully to sleep in the cinema seats. A few days later they were moved on to St Stephen's Church in Walthamstow where she slept on straw. The survivors had no idea what was going to happen next. They couldn't get back to Silvertown and lost their jobs as a result. Their next move was to Finchley Rest Centre. They felt like refugees.

Nina Hibbin remembered how the Blitz survivors had attempted to organize themselves but there was a limit to what they could achieve. They clubbed together to buy first-aid equipment, brought their own folding stools to the tube stations where places were allocated, and older people were given priority. But they could not pump out the wet. There was so much water on the floor that they were wading in it. There were no toilets and only the authorities or the ARP could make any really substantial improvements. The survivors were so angry and desperate that they took a deputation to the ARP, but as they marched towards their headquarters they were charged by mounted police. *They came pouring through the entrance wielding their batons, and I remember one of them got hold of a man with a bandage round his neck and began beating him up. And then a number of people were taken to the police station, and that was the end of our delegation.'*

These glimpses of life in the Blitz are a far cry from the romanticized idea of people 'muddling through' to a background of community singing. Anarchy, looting and fear of civil unrest were prevalent.

Outside the London area, the Chislehurst caves in Kent became a natural shelter. Charlie Draper recalled that when he first went down he was amazed to see what was almost an underground city. He found his grandmother, who had saved him a bunk. They were two-tier bunks and were considered at the time to be luxurious. He visited the caves on a higher level and discovered a dance hall with an old piano where people were sitting having a singsong. There was also a cinema. In the tea room the WVS (Women's Voluntary Service) were selling pies and sandwiches and cakes, and a cup of tea could be bought for a penny. Then further along he came to the hospital where children were lining up to get cough mixture, and there was a small chapel. On Sundays Charlie used to go there to hear children singing hymns. There were even washrooms and separate toilets. *'It was quite nice, I enjoyed it.'*

Slowly, the population began to cope with the bombing. Emily Eary explained that she remembered the 10 May 1941 raid, when the whole of London seemed to be on fire. Her family and friends had been down the tube all night, but when they came out in the morning, they had to run through the fire which was raging on both sides of the streets, with hot embers raining down on them. Strangely, these survivors had actually got used to their daily run. At least they had bunks in the tube, and felt secure there. *'We knew that when we got down there we'd have everything we needed to get by, whatever happened on top, whether there was raging fires or bombs falling.'*

A girl, then aged six, remembered the falling of one particularly terrifying bomb. Earlier she had been listening to the adults in her shelter saying that the raid was exceptionally heavy. *'One night they will get the railway line,'* her mother commented. The railway line was a quarter of a mile away and a target because it carried ammunition trains from the Park Royal factory.

Seconds later there came a tremendous bang, and the lights in their back-garden shelter went out. She fully expected the shelter to collapse, but nothing happened although she could hear the sound of bricks falling, and people yelling.

'We're hit!' screamed her mother, and ran out of the shelter. Her young daughter followed up the ladder towards the searchlights outside to see their hens on fire, cackling and flapping in the distance. They hurried up the back-garden path and through the house just as her uncle came in through the front door.

'*Keep those children in,*' he shouted. But they all ran past him.

On the opposite side of the street was a large hole where two houses had once stood. Bricks were still falling and a ring of wardens kept shouting '*Keep back, keep back!*' to the crowd which was gathering in the semi-darkness.

Mr Leggatt, the owner, was helped out of the ruins of his house, bleeding round the head, followed by his son, with only a scratch on his hand.

After a long time, with planes roaring, bombs falling all round, whistles blowing, searchlights and barrage balloons overhead, the ambulance came. A stretcher was carried out, bearing a blanket covered body. Then another, but with a face showing, covered with blood.

Mrs Leggatt had died, but her daughter,

Margaret, had survived. By a miracle, the Jones family, who lived in the next-door house, were away.

A warden ordered the children indoors as the raid was still continuing, but the crowd were reluctant to disperse, fascinated by their glimpses of life so abruptly interrupted.

Margaret and her father had been folding a tablecloth by the larder door when the blast came. Dozens of jars and bottles had been blown into fragments, and Margaret Leggatt was still having operations five years after the war to remove the glass. She was eighteen in 1941.

The downstairs windows of the six-year-old girl's house were broken, but she remembered that for some reason the upstairs ones were not. The broken glass covered a pot of yellow chrysanthemums and her mother picked out as much as she could. The house was covered in soot and the white Victorian frilled nightie belonging to Precious, her doll, had to be destroyed because it was so filthy. She hated Hitler even more after that traumatic night.

After the bomb site had been cleared, she and her friends would play there and have secret fires. One day a neighbour saw them and said, *'That's where Mrs Leggatt died. You kids ought to be ashamed.'* They never went there to play again, but instead set up a small stone memorial and put flowers on it in summer, leaves in winter, and holly at Christmas.

That Christmas Eve the children secretly returned to the bomb site and sang 'Away in a Manger,' then

'Whistle while you work
Hitler is a twerp
Goering's barmy
So's his army
Whistle while you work.'

Being bombed is brought vividly to life by another young girl from London:

'A nasty nervous feeling in the kitchen. Every thud, Mrs R would say "Is that a bomb?" and Mr R would say, "No, it's a gun, dear." As time went on, they'd said it so often Mr R would answer, "No 'sa gun," then just, "'Sa gun," then finally a noise that sounded like S'gun. She could see he was getting irritated and tried not to do it; muttering the question under her breath instead; which of course made it more irritating still. I felt all swollen up with irritation, bloated, but actually it was fear.'

She went out of the house on a beautiful summer night, made even more beautiful by the red glow from the east, where the docks were burning. She recognized she was watching history and tried to fix the sight in her mind. Sitting with a friend on the long, unkempt grass she saw the searchlights swooping from one end of the sky to the other and thought it was like watching the end of the world.

Two bombs fell in the far distance. Then, suddenly, she heard a weird sound just above the roofs *'as if someone was scratching the sky with a broken fingernail.'* This was followed by a tremendous crash a couple of gardens away and she felt the earth juddering under her.

Panic-stricken, the girl ran towards the house, her friend pulling at her and yelling. She felt a strange feeling around her, and was thrown on her face, just inside the kitchen door. Waves seemed to be buffeting her, one after another, just like bathing in a rough sea, and she clutched at the carpet to prevent herself being swept away. There was the smell of carpet in her nose now and she could hear someone screaming. Her friend had gone and she was plunged into dusty darkness. She still *'clutched the floor as if it was a cliff-face; why I had this feeling of saving myself from falling, I don't know.'* She discovered later that her mouth was full of plaster and dust, but she had no sensation of that at the time. In fact her feelings were almost tranquil. She was in a neighbour's house and she could hear a man yelling, *'Down, everybody, get* down. *Do what I tell you, get your heads down!' Over and over – no sense in it, because we'd had the bomb now and everybody was down, heads and all.'*

Her friend flashed a torch around and she could see plaster and glass everywhere; the whole ceiling had collapsed, burying the furniture, with only a clock and a cushion sticking out. The man was still shouting, giving contradictory instructions, and clearly in shock. *'Don't move, stay where you are! Someone tell them next door. Don't move till I tell you!'*

They stumbled through the debris to the front door. It was wedged tight and wouldn't move, but there were people outside and someone screaming, *'Naomi, ask Naomi, Naomi will know. Has anyone seen Naomi?'*

As there was no way of getting out in this direction, they returned to the front room which was in better condition because the ceiling had held, and eventually they crawled out through a broken window. *'It looked so bright outside I couldn't believe it, a sort of white haze, a halo over everything, though there was no moon. Two of the women cried when they saw us; how terrible we must have looked, smothered in white plaster all over, and streaks of blood from the glass. "Are you hurt... are you all right?" people kept asking. It was only then that it occurred to me I* might *have been hurt – I had been in* actual danger. *Up to that minute I had taken everything for granted, in a queer brainless way, as if it were all perfectly ordinary.'*

CHAPTER 20

CHRIS BONINGTON'S CONQUEST OF EVEREST

Chris Bonington had promised himself, his wife and his two sons, that he would never again attempt to climb Everest. It was a promise he broke. He had to. For Everest is many climbers' ultimate goal and it had to be his. But so many had died on the face of the mountain that those who loved him could not help wondering if he would join them.

A grisly reminder came to him on the descent from his failed 1982 attempt on the peak. Bonington had reached the top of a slope that led down to the Col, when he noticed what he thought was another tent. Unthinkingly he veered towards it, but as he came nearer Bonington saw a woman sitting upright in the snow, her fair hair blowing in the wind. Her teeth, however, were bared in a grimace.

Bonington hurried away, knowing that he had intruded on the dead. The upright corpse must have been the wife of the leader of the German expedition of 1979. Her name was Hannelore Schmatz and she had died of exhaustion on the South East Ridge on her way down. Her body must have been carried on down the face of the mountain by an avalanche which had propped Hannelore up in this grotesquely lifelike position, forever staring ahead, a terrible warning to all mountaineers of the frailty of human life in the struggle to conquer Everest. To reach the summit was a superhuman achievement; to return alive was yet another challenge – denied to many.

Bonington knew what it was like to suffer for the love of climbing mountains. He all too vividly remembered his fight for survival on the descent from the Ogre in the Karakoram range, Pakistan when storms had lashed the desolation and he had broken ribs as well as pneumonia. But the challenge was still stronger than the fear.

In 1979, millionaire businessman Arne Naess contacted Bonington and told him he was putting together a team. Naess had booked Everest for 1985 so that he could lead the first Norwegian expedition to the summit.

Over the intervening period, Bonington and Naess got to know each other and Naess finally asked him if he would like to join his expedition rather than just acting as a consultant. Bonington did not agree immediately. He was making his own attempt on Everest in 1982 and did not want to commit himself to Naess there and then.

Bonington did not reach the summit in 1982 and when his close friends – Peter Boardman and Joe Tasker – died on the mountain he promised never to return to Everest, but in the end, much to his family's consternation but eventual agreement, he joined Naess's expedition. Originally there had been twelve members of the team but two of the most talented climbers died in an abseiling accident.

Bonington writes: *'There are many rituals associated with climbing Everest, and their very familiarity was a reassurance, a series of signposts towards the summit. I enjoyed waking in the dark of the pre-dawn in my own little tent, then going across to the cook's shelter which was so much warmer and cosier than the mess tent. The cooking stoves, which had been lit by one of the cook boys, were standing on a table of piled stones in the middle of the shelter, roaring away under the big detchies [cooking pots]. Ang Tendi, our chief cook, was still in his sleeping bag, curled up on a mattress on top of some boxes at the end of the shelter. Ang Nima, one of the cook boys, poured me a mug of tea and I sat on a box.'*

Bonington ate a plateful of rice covered with dal and red chillies. Sherpas arrived as well as the three other climbers going into the Icefall that day.

There were no commands or conferences and the atmosphere was casual. Eventually, the Sherpas drifted out, picked up their loads and then, pausing at the smouldering fire, muttered a prayer. Tossing on to it a handful of rice they set off in the dim light towards the Icefall. Bonington also prayed that everyone would return safely from the deadly Icefall that day.

The worst section was near the top, where a huge and unstable cliff of ice barred their way. It was about seventy-five yards high, and the only way to avoid this sinister obstacle was to climb through a canyon filled with ice blocks. Halfway along the canyon protruded a huge fin of ice and Bonington decided to take the narrow passage behind it. This was about five yards long and only 'shoulder' width. He had just gone a short way in when he heard a sharp crack, abruptly followed by a dull and heavy crunching sound.

Glancing round, Bonington saw that the fin had suddenly broken off at its base and completely closed the passage. A few seconds earlier, he would have been sliced in two by the razor-sharp edge of ice.

He was very shaken. It was as if the mountain had closed in on him, its brute force compelling him to continue. Who was in control? Everest or Bonington?

The expedition was now ready to make its first camp. Because Bonington did not speak Norwegian, all important conversations were held in English. Arne Naess had no time for formal meetings, but used mealtimes for discussion and planning. He put up ideas and listened to suggestions, but he always made the final decision, thus retaining control. With the exception of

Christian Larsson, Naess was the least experienced mountaineer in the team, but nevertheless Bonington regarded him as a good leader, with charisma, an excellent sense of humour and a quick analytical mind.

Naess later announced that because of the dangers of the Icefield, he proposed keeping all the Sherpa force at Base Camp until they had ferried supplies for the climb up to Camp 1. Bonington could see the logic behind all this but he was not happy with the plan, preferring to divide the Sherpa teams between the camps from the beginning. This would ensure a stream of supplies was always just behind the climbers, which he considered psychologically vital. It would also mean the expedition would be making maximum use of the good weather they had at the moment.

Bonington had a wakeful night, knowing that Naess currently had a throat infection. Could it be this that was affecting the Norwegian's judgement? Bonington decided to make some calculations.

He had brought with him a computer that was powered by batteries and a solar panel. He used it for writing reports and letters as well as for solving logistical problems. Next morning he switched on the computer, and using the spreadsheet began to calculate the difference between Naess's plan and his own in terms of feasibility and efficiency. Bonington then went over to Naess's tent and explained his findings – that they should be able to station a Sherpa team at Camp 1 directly they had opened the route to Camp 2. Bonington suggested that he himself should move up to Camp 1 so that he could supervise the flow of supplies through to Camp 2. Naess immediately agreed to compromise, an incident that underlines the great potential for success the expedition had. Chris Bonington and Arne Naess were able to work together – as did the other members of this highly sophisticated team of climbers, its back-up managers and helpers and Sherpas.

The decision had been taken that once the three climbers out in front had reached the next part of the ascent of Everest, where they planned to set up Camp 3, Bonington and his two Norwegian team mates, Odd Eliassen and Bjorn Myrer-Lund, would take the route to the South Col. They would then put the other three into the right position to make the first assault on the summit. As this was a Norwegian expedition, Bonington had realized the final ascent would be made by an all-Norwegian group.

Bonington was also concerned about his own stamina. He was 50, and worried about burning himself out.

On 3 April, accompanied by Bjorn and Odd,

Bonington moved up to Camp 2. It was already a small village of tents, sadly littered with the debris of other expeditions. This was becoming a real problem on the slopes of Everest. Several large expeditions were visiting the mountain each year, not only leaving mounds of rubbish but also polluting the water supplies. The Norwegian expedition had already suffered at Camp 1 from a form of dysentery called jardia. Bonington was certain that this was caused by the melted snow that formed their water supplies being polluted from the latrines of other expeditions.

As they moved up the Lhotse Face, over a thousand yards of steep bare ice leading up to the South Col, they came to the South-West Face and the site of Bonington's Camp 4 of some years ago. It was an eerie sight, with boxes specially designed by Hamish MacInnes still clinging to the slope.

At Camp 2, the expedition doctor checked the three of them over and decided that Odd's blood had dangerously thickened and he needed to lose altitude fast. Deeply disappointed, he was forced to descend, and the next morning Bjorn and Chris Bonington, together with two Sherpas, Ang Rita and Sundhare, set out for Camp 3, sleeping that night on oxygen.

Next day, Bonington had to struggle with his oxygen system. Frustratingly, the straps of his mask were the wrong length and he couldn't fasten one of the buckles. Losing his temper, he flung the mask into the snow only to see the other climbers vanishing round the corner. He felt exhausted already. The night on oxygen had done him little good, and, retrieving the mask, he struggled on behind his companions. Arriving at a steep if small step he noticed they hadn't bothered to put a fixed rope on it. He cursed them, cursed the mountain and cursed the whole expedition.

The snout of his oxygen mask was making it impossible to look down, so traversing the slope was difficult. By now, Sundhare and Ang Rita were no more than little dots on the other side of the sweep of ice leading to the broken limestone rocks known as the Yellow Band. Bjorn was already halfway across the ice slope on his way to join them.

The next day both Bjorn and Chris Bonington had dysentery, but in a radio call Arne Naess still urged them to continue.

In fact, Chris Bonington's summit bid did not come for some days and he returned to the Base Camp to prepare for the vital climb while another team attempted an ascent. After some rest, he was ready to try for the ascent. The second summit team was composed of Bjorn Myrer-Lund, Pertemba, Odd Eliassen and Chris Bonington, who writes: *'There are many parallels between climbing a mountain and fighting a war. This is perhaps why the vocabulary is very similar – assault, siege, logistics.'*

It could be said that the danger involved in climbing the higher Himalayan peaks is greater than that encountered in some wartime battles. The casualty figures speak for that. Bonington considered the spirit of climbing, however, rather different. *'The climber is working with, and through, the natural forces. He doesn't fight the storm; he works his way through it, perhaps shelters from it.'*

The real link to war strategy comes where a climb is big enough to use set camps and a support team. No matter how talented the lead climbers are, if their supplies don't reach them, they would have to retreat, just as a military advance can also be halted through lack of fuel or ammunition.

The date was 18 April 1985, and the second summit team set out before dawn, discovering that near the top of the Icefall there had been yet another collapse and what had been a difficult walk over piled blocks was now a deep valley. Worse still, the ladders that had been placed there the previous day were down amongst the rubble, broken and useless.

The Sherpas were already busy trying to rebuild some kind of route, and Bonington clambered up to what appeared to be a ledge but what was actually a sharply honeycombed fin with deep crevasses on either side. As he edged across it an ice block broke away beneath him and fell into the depths below, clattering and bouncing in the most terrifying way, and he froze, knowing that he could so easily have gone with it.

The team arrived at Camp 1 with the unsettling but adrenalin-making knowledge that the next day, 19 April, was to bring their challenge for the summit.

They made a relaxed start. Bonington walked steadily but slowly, falling behind the others but this time not worrying too much because he wanted to pace himself rather than making the mistake of allowing himself to feel insecure. Once on the fixed ropes he maintained a steady rhythm, kicking crampon points into the hard ice and then measuring the excruciatingly slow progress upwards against landmarks that had become all too familiar, such as a rock sticking out of the ice and the foot of the Geneva Spur. Their objective was hidden by a great plume of cloud that covered the summit.

Bonington was just short of Camp 3 when he saw a figure descending the fixed ropes from above. He recognized Ralph Hoibakk from the first summit team. They had been defeated by gales and were forced to return. This meant that Bonington's team now stood the chance of making the first ascent for the expedition. But to him, this was not the challenge at all. Reaching the summit of Everest was a personal goal.

Next morning the team climbed the fixed rope to the South Col. There were no clouds and it was less windy. Once there, Chris Bonington was again saddened to see the debris of other expeditions – old tents, food boxes, oxygen bottles, the scattered litter of other warriors in their grim fight with the mountain.

Bonington had a comparatively sleepless night and woke early to make sure he was fully prepared for this momentous day. Two hours later the team was ready, with their bulbous clothing and oxygen equipment, accompanied by the Sherpas. The time was 1:30 am when they set out across the Col, their crampons slipping and catching on the stone underfoot. Slowly they made their way to a bulge of hard smooth ice whose angle increased as they approached the ridge.

Each team member followed the light cast by his head-torch. Bonington was bringing up the rear and it wasn't long before Pertemba, at the front of the column, had considerably widened the gap. They were now on a snow slope reaching up into the broken rocks that guarded the base of the ridge. The scrambling was comparatively easy but still tense in the dark with all their weighty high-altitude gear.

Bonington felt exhausted again, finding it increasingly hard to place one foot in front of the other. He had dropped even further behind the others. When he caught up after they had stopped for a rest they got up and started off again. Bonington slumped into the snow, involuntarily muttering that he would never make it. Hearing him, Odd firmly told him that he would. He also volunteered to stay behind with him. Odd had just been cleared by the doctor, although he was fully aware of how dangerous thickening of the blood was at these heights.

They had begun the ascent in darkness but now a grey dawn was beginning to break. *'The soaring peak of the South Summit was touched with gold as the sun swept over the horizon far to the east,'* Bonington remembered.

By the time the team had reached the crest which had been the site of the Hillary and Tenzing (the first conquerors of Everest in 1953) top camp, the peaks around them were gloriously lit by the sun's low-flung rays.

It was now 5 in the morning and they were at 27,000 feet. The going was much harder than Bonington had ever imagined. The wind was getting up again but they had reached the South Summit. The question now was whether or not they had enough oxygen to get back. The others had been using three litres a minute, but Bonington had switched to four. He would have even less reserves, but he was determined to continue.

Roped together, he and Odd began the final ascent of the summit, the others having vanished round the corner. The ascent eased slightly and suddenly Bonington realized that all he had to do was put one foot in front of the other for that last stretch to the highest point on earth. It was an incredible feeling of relief.

Suddenly he had arrived. Everest dropped away below him, and he hugged Pertemba who was now crouching beside him. The actual summit was roughly the size of a pool table, but they found they could all move about without fear of falling over the edge. Soon, Odd and Bjorn, who were raising and photographing the Norwegian flag, came over and embraced him.

They remained on the summit, lost in wonder at the view, hardly able to believe they had made it at last.

Around them lay the Tibetan plateau, hundreds of brown hills with the occasional white cap. To the east rose Kangchenjunga, first climbed by George Band and Joe Brown in 1955, and to the west the great chain of the Himalayas, with Shisha Pangma, China's 26,000-feet peak, on the horizon. Doug Scott, Alex McIntyre and Roger Baxter-Jones had climbed its South Face in 1982. Immediately below them, just the other side of the Western Cwm, was Nuptse, looking stunted, the very reverse of the view that Bonington had enjoyed twenty-four years earlier, when Everest had seemed so far out of his reach. To the south were dense clouds covering the foothills and plains of India. They had arrived on top of the world and they were all still alive.

To make this achievement at 50 was a considerable feat and the fulfilment of a personal quest. Bonington never sought glory but only personal satisfaction at finally attaining the pinnacle of his climbing career.

CHAPTER 21

COLLISION AT SEA

The sinking of the *Andrea Doria* in July 1956 was the worst peacetime shipping disaster since the loss of the *Titanic* in 1912. Although casualties were in fact lighter – 44 killed on the *Andrea Doria* and 3 on the *Stockholm,* the ship she collided with – if the rescue had been less effective the death toll could have been much higher.

The *Andrea Doria* was the flagship of the Italian Line, a strikingly beautiful luxury liner, opulently furnished with murals and paintings throughout her public rooms. She was 690 feet long, had a gross registered tonnage of 29,083 tonnes and a cruising speed of 22 knots. At the time of the collision, the *Andrea Doria* was carrying 190 first-class, 267 cabin-class and 672 tourist-class passengers. She also had 70 crew members.

The *Andrea Doria* left for her cruise from her home port of Genoa and called at Naples, Cannes and Gibraltar. She was due to dock in New York on 25 July 1956, and was on the usual tight schedule for this kind of ship. The passengers had to be pleased, there must be no complaints and the owners wanted the Captain to make sure that all ran smoothly. Captain Calamai's plan had been to make for the *Nantucket* lightship on the approach to New York and then pass south of her.

The *Stockholm,* a Swedish-built liner, was sailing from New York on 25 July and she also intended to pass close to the south of the lightship. Add to these two intentions thick and blanketing fog, and the scenario had already been written for one of the worst disasters ever known at sea

The *Andrea Doria* ran into the fog when she was 150 miles from the *Nantucket* lightship. The usual precautions were taken, such as sounding the siren, closing the watertight doors and posting look-outs. The ship's navigational radar was switched on and seemed to be working perfectly and a 5 per cent reduction in speed was made, from 22 to 21 knots. The anti-collision rules at that time insisted ships must proceed at a moderate speed in fog, and defined 'moderate' as the speed at which the vessel could be stopped within the visibility distance. Twenty-one knots could certainly not be called a moderate speed, but many passenger liners didn't comply, largely because their captains were desperate to keep to the schedules and minimize any complaints from the all-powerful passengers. Calamai was no exception. He had decided to rely on his radar.

At dusk, visibility was down to half a mile and there were three echoes showing on the *Doria's* radar. One was astern and two ahead, but all of them were going in the same direction as the *Andrea Doria*. Calamai kept a close scrutiny on the two echoes ahead but at 21 knots his ship overtook them. Just before 21.30 another small echo appeared on the screen, but the captain soon realized that this was stationary and therefore bound to be the *Nantucket* lightship.

At approximately 22.45, the Officer of the

Watch, Second Officer Francini, noticed another echo on the radar screen that was almost dead ahead, slightly off the starboard bow and rapidly closing. Calamai double-checked the radar screen himself. Francini was right. The object was on the starboard bow and steering a course roughly the same as the *Andrea Doria*. Calamai thought that they would pass starboard to starboard and he considered this too close. He altered course 4 degrees to port to widen the distance, telling the helmsman to steer 'nothing to starboard'. By giving this order he broke the Rule of the Road. This states that when two ships are meeting bow on, or nearly bow on, they should both alter course to starboard. If one ship believes she can avoid an incident by a timely alteration of course, any such alteration must be decisive and early. Unfortunately, Calamai's decision was neither of these.

The Officer of the Watch on the *Stockholm*, Third Officer Carstens, told the subsequent enquiry that when he had first picked up the *Andrea Doria's* echo, it was not on the *Stockholm's* starboard bow but was fine on her port bow. He made the decision that the two ships were going to meet nearly bow on and that if there was to be any alteration to the *Stockholm's* course, it must be to starboard.

Although opinions differ, it would appear that

the *Andrea Doria* and the *Stockholm* were now approximately between three and a half to five miles apart and Calamai was becoming increasingly worried that the two ships must be getting close, despite the fact that he had not heard the other vessel's fog signal. He had very little time left to take any more avoiding action. With a relative approach speed of 40 knots there were between three and four minutes to go.

Calamai had been expecting to see a green starboard light on their starboard bow and ordered a close look-out. Then, to his alarm, he saw a red port light instead and realized the *Stockholm* appeared to be crossing their bows. He gave the order to go hard to port and sounded two blasts on the siren. But he was already too late.

As the *Andrea Doria* started to turn the *Stockholm's* bow hit her, crashing into her starboard side abreast of the bridge.

The *Stockholm* had sailed from New York at 11.30, following the French liner, *Île de France,* down the Hudson River towards the open sea. The weather was hot, with a light haze, and the *Île de France* slowly drew ahead of the *Stockholm.* At 20.00 hours, when Third Officer Carstens came on watch, the visibility was still reasonably good. Captain Nordensen came up on the bridge at 21.00 for about half an hour and ordered a 3-degree alteration of course from 090 degrees to 087 degrees. This was to avoid passing the *Nantucket* lightship at too great a distance. He then went to his cabin, leaving orders to be called if there was fog, if another ship came within a mile, and when the *Nantucket* was abeam.

Carstens then checked the *Stockholm's* position by radio bearings and found that a northerly set was taking the ship too far to the north. He made a 2-degree alteration to 089 degrees to allow for this. At about 23.00 hours he took another fix and discovered that the ship was still too far northwards so he altered her course to 091 degrees. The decision had been to pass close to the south of the *Nantucket* and this was Carstens' objective.

Soon afterwards, a radar echo appeared on his screen at a range of 12 miles and then at 10, all of which he recorded in the log. The weather was still clear and Carstens saw no reason to reduce his speed, which was about 18 knots. He didn't realize the *Andrea Doria* was in fog until just before the collision.

Carstens posted a look-out on the port side of the bridge with clear instructions to let him know immediately he saw lights. Carstens had also decided that as soon as he saw any lights himself, he would alter course to starboard as he believed the two ships were approaching roughly bow on.

But he saw nothing, and as a result became increasingly concerned. Then the bridge look-out reported 'lights to port', and at the same time the crow's nest did the same. Carstens went to the wing of the bridge and saw the two masthead lights of the *Andrea Doria,* very close but still to port. He told the helmsman to take the *Stockholm* 20 degrees to starboard, then ordered 'midships', followed by 'steady as you go'. Interrupted by a telephone call to the bridge from the crow's nest, Carstens quickly returned to the port wing and saw to his horror that the *Andrea Doria* was even closer and he could now see her green starboard light. It was too late for the *Stockholm* too. Devastated, Carstens realized the *Andrea Doria* could not be passing him port to port as he had thought, but appeared to be actually crossing his bow. He immediately ordered hard astern, and then full astern. Then the *Stockholm's* bow hit the *Andrea Doria,* slicing into her.

As no order on board the *Andrea Doria* had been given to stop engines, she was still travelling quite fast. Because of this, she shook the bows of the *Stockholm* clear which then scraped down her side, causing considerable damage and an amazing shower of sparks. The *Stockholm's* engines had already been stopped.

Eventually both ships came to a standstill. The

Stockholm lost all her anchor cables but not her two anchors which had become entangled in the wreckage. Her cables, however, caught in a sea-bed obstruction and anchored her.

At this stage, neither ship knew the identity of the other. The *Stockholm* broadcast on the distress frequency that she had been in collision with an unknown vessel. Virtually at the same time, the *Andrea Doria* also made a distress signal and the Stockholm was therefore able to identify her.

The Italian liner was crippled. The *Stockholm* had hit her in the starboard fuel tanks. These were virtually empty and the ocean rushed in. The *Stockholm* was badly damaged, with her bows stove in, pushed back by about 60 feet, and her forward crew mess desk had been virtually obliterated. Nevertheless, because her forward bulkhead was holding up well, she was still afloat.

The order was given on the *Andrea Doria* for the port lifeboats to be swung out, but she was now listing to starboard so badly that they couldn't be lowered. A number of ships began to sail to the disaster area, but while on the *Stockholm* no passengers had been killed, on the *Andrea Doria* the casualty list was high.

The *Île de France* returned from the Atlantic, arriving on the scene at 02.00 hours, taking up her position on the stricken *Andrea Doria's* starboard side. About 1,500 passengers remained aboard her, the others having been transferred to the *Stockholm* and to the *Cape Ann* in the lifeboats that could be launched.

The passengers still on the *Andrea Doria* were assembled on the high port side and assisted down the steep slope of the deck to the low, side where ropes and ladders helped them to the waiting lifeboats. Nets were used to lower any handicapped or elderly passengers. By now, over thirty boats had arrived on the scene, and they formed a flotilla, ferrying passengers to the *Île de France*, the *Stockholm,* a US Navy transport and the *Cape Ann*. A destroyer escort eventually took on board Captain Calamai and his officers, but not until the very end of the rescue operation. Although considerable efforts went into trying to keep the *Andrea Doria* afloat, she eventually sank.

Movingly, as she left at the end of the rescue, the *Île de France* circled the area where the *Andrea Doria* had gone down, half-masted her colours, sounded her siren and dipped her ensign. She returned to New York with the survivors, as did all the other rescue craft.

One young survivor had an unbelievably lucky escape. Linda Morgan was fourteen and had been asleep in a cabin on the *Andrea Doria* with her sister while their parents were in the cabin next door. The bow of the *Stockholm* actually smashed its way into her cabin, going underneath Linda and depositing her on the forecastle of the *Stockholm* behind a kind of breakwater which was about two and a half feet high and about eighty feet from the *Stockholm's* bows. Because of this she was protected.

She was found by a Spanish sailor and his two Swedish companions. Piteously, Linda spoke to him in Spanish asking, *'Donde esta Mama'*, (where is mother?). She had been born in Mexico and Spanish was still her first language. At first the sailor naturally assumed Linda Morgan was amongst the passengers on the *Stockholm*, but when he checked there was no such person listed.

Eventually, to everyone's amazement, it was discovered that she had been literally plucked out of the *Doria* by the *Stockholm*, and when the two ships broke apart she remained on board the *Stockholm*.

The two shipping lines sued each other, but eventually decided to settle out of court.

In such a large-scale disaster it was a miracle that so many passengers survived.

CHAPTER 22

CANNIBALISM
IN THE ANDES

The Fairchild F-227 belonging to the Uruguayan Air Force had been chartered by an amateur rugby team and was scheduled to fly from Montevideo, Uruguay, to Santiago, Chile. The date was 12 October 1972.

Because of bad weather in the Andes, the plane touched down in Mendoza, which was on the Argentinian side of the mountains.

Next day, however, conditions had improved sufficiently to allow the Fairchild to fly on. At 3.21 p.m., the pilot reported to Air Traffic Control in Santiago that he was over the Planchon Pass and later, at 3.24 p.m., he was flying over the town of Curico in Chile.

Authorized to turn north, he began his descent to the airport of Pudahuel. At 3.30 p.m., the pilot reported that he was now flying at 15,000 feet. When Santiago Air Traffic Control contacted him again, there was no response. The Fairchild had vanished.

The search, which involved Uruguayans, Argentinians and Chileans, lasted for eight days but nothing was found, which is hardly surprising in such a vast mountain range where, in early spring, there had been heavy falls of snow. Fatally, the top of the plane was painted white. The assumption was made that the pilot had miscalculated, the aircraft had crashed into a white wilderness and there could be no possible hope for the forty-five passengers and crew.

The passenger list included twenty-five friends and relations as well as the fifteen members of the rugby team, all from some of Uruguay's most eminent families.

The team had been Christian Brother educated and belonged to the Old Christians' Club whose main activity was to play rugby on a Sunday afternoon. The atmosphere was jovial in the passenger compartment of the Fairchild as the plane neared its destination: a rugby ball was being passed up and down the cabin, a group were playing cards. A steward advised everyone that there was some bad weather ahead but there was nothing to be concerned about, immediately resuming his own game of cards with the navigator.

As the plane ploughed into a cloud bank there were nervous jokes that petered out when the Fairchild hit an air pocket and dropped several hundred feet. The clarity returned as they emerged from the cloud bank. But what clarity! All the passengers could see was a snow covered mountain which was only about ten feet from the tip of the wing.

The pilot tried desperately to make the Fairchild climb and some passengers, instantly aware of the danger, began to pray.

For a moment they wondered if the plane might make it, but then the Fairchild's starboard wing hit the side of the mountain, breaking off, somersaulting over the fuselage and snapping off the tail. Some of the passengers were catapulted out. Within seconds the port wing broke away and a propeller blade cut into the fuselage.

Then the miracle happened.

Rather than smashing into the side of the mountain, what was left of the fuselage landed right way up in the snow of a steep valley and slid for hundreds of feet.

The wrecked plane hit the ground at about 200 knots, and a further two passengers were sucked out of the rear as the Fairchild continued to slide downhill. Seats broke away from their mountings, freezing Andes air rushed into the decompressed cabin, but the fuselage slid on, showing no sign of breaking up. Then it slowed and came to a halt on a slight rise facing down the valley. It was bitterly cold and the survivors were only wearing blazers or sports jackets.

In a state of shock, two third-year medical students tried to help the injured and dying, but there was little they could do and the thin air of the Andes made their attempts doubly difficult.

The crash had occurred at about 3 o'clock in the afternoon. By four, it was beginning to snow. The plane's radio was not working and the survivors who could walk went out into the snow, fearing the plane might yet explode or catch fire.

Thirty-two passengers escaped with their lives, and those that could stood outside, staring at the forbidding landscape, the last place on earth where they could make any attempt at survival.

When night came they returned to the wreckage of the plane, but there was very little space to stand and certainly none to lie down. The jagged break at the back of the fuselage had left seven windows on the left hand side of the plane and four on the right. The most seriously injured had been laid in a clear space by the entrance, and although they were at least horizontal, there was hardly any protection from the snow and the bitter mountain wind. One survivor, Marcelo Perez, aided by the well-built Roy Harley, had tried to make some kind of protective barrier for them with seats and suitcases, but the wind was so strong that it kept falling down.

The night passed with extreme difficulty, the uninjured drinking the wine the dead pilots had bought in Mendoza and hoping that the alcohol would fortify them against the cold, the wind and the desolation of their predicament. One survivor discovered that the upholstery in the seats could be removed and used as inadequate blankets. It was the first of many improvisations.

Those who were not drunk were hysterical, and the cries of the injured were dreadful to hear. In the morning, three of them were dead. The only surviving crew member checked the supplies only to discover that most of the alcoholic drink had been consumed and the only food for the surviving twenty-eight people was eight bars of chocolate, five bars of nougat, scattered caramels, dates and dried plums, a packet of salted biscuits, two tins of mussels, one tin of salted almonds, and a small jar each of peach, apple and blackberry jam. Marcelo Perez, now self-elected leader, served lunch to each survivor – a square of chocolate and wine in a cap from a deodorant can.

That afternoon a plane flew overhead but

before nightfall another of the injured had died. Next morning, the sky was clear and the survivors hoped for rescue, but in the meantime they had to cope with thirst. It was difficult to melt the snow quickly enough and eating the excruciatingly cold stuff was painful. Someone suggested either compressing the snow into a ball of ice and sucking it, or cramming it into a bottle and shaking it until the snow melted. In the end, Fito Strauch came up with an invention – a water-making device powered by harnessing solar heat. Using a rectangle of aluminium foil that came from the inside of a broken seat, he bent the sides to form a shallow bowl and twisted one corner to make a spout. He then covered it thinly with snow and tilted his machine so that it faced the sun. Slowly, drops of water appeared in the spout, and then a steady trickle filled a bottle that Fito held underneath. Some of the others began to follow his example, and Marcelo then organized the survivors into different groups: a medical team, a cabin team and water makers.

Another plane flew over them, but despite desperate shouting and waving they were unable to attract its attention.

By Monday morning there was still no sign of rescue, but the condition of some of the injured had improved. Getting back to civilization through their own efforts was discussed, but it was decided there was simply not enough food to sustain the expedition. It was then that one survivor said that he would 'cut meat from one of the pilots. After all, they got us into this mess.

At the time no one took him seriously.

Looking at the charts from the pilots' cabin, the survivors decided that they must be in Chile, on the western side of the Andes. One of the pilots had repeatedly said they were past Curico which was well into Chile. The needle on the plane's altimeter pointed to 7,000 feet and Chilean villages must be somewhere to the west. The main problem, however, was that they were blocked in by mountains and they would have to climb to the west to reach safety.

The inventor, Fito, worked out that if passenger seat cushions were tied to their feet, they would act as snowshoes, and at 7 o'clock on the morning of Tuesday, 17 October, four of the survivors set out on a reconnaissance expedition. They walked for an hour in the bitter cold and then took a rest, tying on the cushions over rugby boots. Unfortunately, this meant one foot stepping on the other and the expedition was forced to walk bow-legged. As none of them had eaten anything that could possibly promote energy, they soon decided to turn back. Without proper food they would never reach civilization.

Then someone raised the point that had been

made earlier. How about eating one of the pilots?

The thought of consuming a fellow human being produced an instinctive revulsion, a built-in disgust. Cannibals have become jokes, clichés in which a white man sits in a cooking pot surrounded by gyrating natives. Never, of course, the other way about. Yet who knows what any of us would do if we were not only starving but desperately needed physical energy as a means of escape?

On the tenth day, 22 October, there was still no sign of rescue. Roy Harley, however, had discovered a transistor radio between two of the seats, and, having a basic knowledge of electronics, had made an aerial with strands of wire taken from the plane's electrical circuits. They could now pick up scraps of news but no indication of any rescue operation.

The limited food supplies were fast running out, and although lichen had been sampled as a possible source of nourishment, the plant was soon rejected because of its bitter taste.

Gradually the survivors realized the worst: to survive they would *have* to eat the bodies of the dead. A meeting was called and they discussed the ramifications of what they were going to do. They reasoned that by now the souls would have left the bodies of those who had died. It was also the moral obligation of the survivors to live for their own sakes as well as for the sakes of their families. Marcelo was still holding back, but the general feeling was to go ahead.

Now the moment could be put off no longer. One of the survivors, Canessa, went over to the bodies that were covered by snow. The buttocks of one of them were exposed and Canessa bared the flesh, hacking the frozen carcass with a piece of broken glass. Eventually, after a good deal of hard work, he cut away twenty extremely thin pieces and put them up on the roof of the plane to dry out in the sun.

When the meat had thawed, however, everyone shrank from taking the first bite, so Canessa forced himself to show an example. After a terrible struggle, he pushed the meat into his mouth and swallowed.

The most emotive description of this appalling but necessary act is contained in a letter from the 24-year-old Gustavo Nicolich to his girlfriend in Montevideo.

Most dear Rosina:

I am writing to you from inside the plane (our petit hotel *for a moment). It is sunset and has started to be rather cold and windy which it usually does at this hour of the evening. Today the weather was wonderful – a beautiful sun and very hot. It reminded me of the days on the beach with you – the big difference being that then we would be going to have lunch at your place at midday whereas now I'm stuck outside the plane without any food at all.*

Today, on top of everything else, it was rather depressing and a lot of the others began to get discouraged (today is the tenth day we have been here), but luckily the gloom did not spread to me because I get incredible strength just by thinking that I'm going to see you again. Another of the things leading to the general depression is that in a while the food will run out: we have only got two tins of seafood (small), one bottle of white wine, and a little cherry brandy left, which for twenty-six men (well, there are also boys who want to be men) is nothing.

One thing that will seem incredible to you – it seems unbelievable to me – is that today we started to cut up the dead in order to eat them.'

Gustavo went on to tell Rosina that he felt there was nothing else he could have done. He had prayed to God to avoid such a decision, but he knew he had to face it with courage and faith. Gustavo had come to the conclusion that the bodies were there because God had put them there and, since the only thing that mattered was the soul, he didn't have to feel great remorse; if his own body had to be eaten eventually, he would be glad if it would save another life.

Listening to the radio, Roy and Marcelo discovered that the search for the missing plane had been called off. Now it was up to the survivors to make their own escape. The human meat was going to become even more necessary. Now most were prepared to eat human flesh, and Canessa and Fito Strauch went back to the corpse and cut off more slivers of meat. Some people, however, still couldn't bring themselves to touch it.

Another reconnaissance was set up and three survivors followed the trail of the plane, hoping to find the tail but discovering instead a number of bodies. They endured a freezing night and had to pummel each other to stay warm. When they returned to the plane, the others were appalled at their physical condition. If one night in the open was going to do that to them, then what hope did they all really have of escape?

Next morning, for the first time, the survivors managed to make a fire with some old Coca Cola crates. They roasted their human meat over the fire, thus making it more acceptable, softer than beef but with a similar taste. Still some refused but they were growing weaker each day.

On the seventeenth day, the teams in and around the wrecked aircraft were working well, melting snow, cutting, cooking and cleaning the interior of the plane. That night, however, disaster struck again when an avalanche fell on what remained of the aircraft, filling the improvised living accommodation with snow. Marcelo died. So did seven others. Now the survivors were reduced to nineteen. Some of these wished they had died like the others as they managed to clamber into the tilted pilots' cabin, only to discover a blizzard was raging outside which was to last some days.

As there was no way of drying or cooking the human flesh, the remaining survivors were forced to eat it raw and some were unable to bring themselves to do so. As a result, their condition worsened.

After more days and nights of appalling suffering, three of the fittest men decided to make a reconnaissance trip as well as making another attempt to find the missing tail section of the Fairchild. After walking for half an hour, they discovered the rear door of the plane and later the scattered contents of the galley, which included an almost empty jar of coffee with a few grains at the bottom, broken sweets, a cylinder of gas, a broken thermos, some maté, and Coca Cola. These remnants made them highly elated, but progress returning to the plane was very difficult as they continually sank up to their knees in deep snow. Eventually they got back, exhausted and realizing that chances of escape were only very slim.

After much discussion it was decided to wait for better weather. During the waiting period the three expeditionaries, Canessa, Vizintin and Parrado, ate more meat and got as fit as was possible in the circumstances. A sledge was made up from half a Samsonite suitcase in which were four rugby socks filled with meat, a bottle of water and cushions for snowshoes. Canessa was in the lead, Vizintin came next, laden with blankets, and Parrado brought up the rear.

The expedition headed towards the north-east which was downhill at the beginning. After a couple of hours' hard walking they at last discovered the tail cone of the Fairchild in which to their joy they found some sugar and three meat pasties. They wolfed the pasties down immediately. There was also rum, cigarettes, woollen socks and clothing.

The expedition made a fire, roasted some human meat and finished off the meal with a spoonful of sugar mixed with toothpaste in half an inch of rum. The sweetness was delicious.

Using the tail as a camp, they spent a comfortable night. The following night in the open, however, was freezing and they had to lie on top of each other to achieve even a minimum warmth. Once again, after much debate, they decided to turn back, but first they would return to the tail and remove some batteries they had discovered. With these it was possible they could make the radio work. To their dismay, the batteries were too heavy to carry. The expedition also took the many cartons of cigarettes to be shared out amongst the other survivors.

The expedition also left messages in the tail of the Fairchild, writing neatly in nail polish:

GO UP.
EIGHTEEN PEOPLE STILL ALIVE.

While the survivors were delighted to receive the returning expedition and its bounty, they knew their chances of rescue now depended on making the radio work. They also realized they would have to transport it back to the tail because the batteries were too heavy to be returned to the remainder of the fuselage. In the interim, another survivor died.

Most of the food-source bodies had been buried by the avalanche and now they had to dig for them. All survivors were now not only desperate for salt but for a different taste. Guarding against the inevitable shortage of bodies, no pilfering was allowed and originally rejected parts of the bodies had to be eaten.

The work on the radio, now in the tail of the plane, was progressing. Eventually it worked and to their joy they discovered the search was to be resumed by a Douglas C-47 of the Uruguayan Air Force. A large cross was made by the tail of the Fairchild, composed of scattered suitcases.

On 12 December, after another survivor had died and the remainder had become depressed, giving up hope, Canessa, Parrado and Vizintin set out again with much more clothing and a larger sleeping bag, determined that the melting snows and better weather would give them the breakthrough that was needed. They took with them a substantial supply of human flesh.

Thirteen survivors remained behind in the fuselage of the plane.

The expedition, meanwhile, thought they saw a road, but when they had ascended a peak, all they could see were limitless mountains. Rather than all three returning, however, the decision was taken to send Vizintin back so that food supplies could be conserved, giving Canessa and Parrado more of a chance to reach civilization. But their progress was slow, their loads heavier as they clambered painfully over the mountains, sliding down the sides, knowing that one false move would kill them.

Then, after almost giving up several times, the much longed-for miracle finally occurred. At the end of a valley they saw a view that was justly akin to paradise. The snow had stopped and from under its mantle flowed a torrent of water that rushed into a gorge. Better still, everywhere Canessa and Parrado gazed, they saw moss, grass, gorse and yellow and purple flowers. They were reaching safety. They both prayed aloud, thanking God, the tears running down their cheeks.

But the ordeal was not entirely over; three men on horseback rode on without acknowledging them, despite their desperate waving. Canessa and Parrado didn't despair. They knew now they were within an ace of rescue. Eventually they made contact with a peasant on the other side of the gorge who wrote a message wrapped around a stone that he threw across the river to them. It read: *'There is a man coming later that I told him to go. Tell me what you want.'*

Parrado and Canessa had not realized what terrifying figures they cut with long hair and beards, wearing their many layers of oddly assorted and adapted clothing.

Parrado wrote back: *'I come from a plane that fell in the mountains. I am Uruguayan. We have been walking for ten days. I have a friend up there who is injured. In the plane there are still fourteen injured people. We have to get out of here quickly and we don't know how. We don't have any food. We are weak. When are you going to come and fetch us? Please. We can't even walk. Where are we?'*

He added in lipstick an SOS and threw the message back across the river wrapped round the stone.

They were eventually rescued by the village people, fed and allowed to sleep. It was now mid-day on Thursday, 21 December, seventy days since the Fairchild had crashed. Meanwhile, one of the peasant farmers rode to the police station, a day's ride away. Eventually the remainder of the survivors were rescued by helicopter from the fuselage of the plane.

Gradually, in the days that followed the rescue, rumour and then admittance of cannibalism was much debated by the media and the Catholic church which, despite the repugnance of many, made supportive comments about the actions of the survivors.

The Andean Rescue Corps and a Catholic priest visited the site of the crash on 18 January 1973, collected the bodies and dug a grave in a place that was protected from avalanches. A stone altar was built above the grave and an iron cross was placed over it. After the service, they splashed petrol over the fuselage of the Fairchild and the wreckage began to burn.

CHAPTER 23

ANNE FRANK'S SAFE HOUSE

One of the most moving stories about a family's desperate bid for survival must be the one so faithfully recorded by Anne Frank.

Anne was a German Jewess whose parents had emigrated to Holland from Germany in 1933. By 1942, they were horrified at Hitler's growing persecution of the Jews, but Anne, at thirteen, had accepted the restricted life she led. She wore a yellow star on her coat, and was not allowed to enter a cinema or a tram and was forbidden to ride a bicycle or even sit out in the garden after eight. Too young to rebel against these ludicrous and humiliating rules, Anne simply made them part of the framework of her life.

A few weeks after her thirteenth birthday, the deportation of the Jews to Auschwitz and other death camps began, and knowing that he and his family could soon be taken, Anne's father, Otto Frank, contrived a highly dangerous but extremely clever plan to hide his family and others until the war was over.

Otto Frank spent some months making his preparations. His firm's office was an old building in Amsterdam which had rooms at the back that overlooked a courtyard – rooms that could be shut off. He chose the two upper back floors to be converted into a hiding place for himself, his wife and two daughters, Anne and her older sister

Margot, and some business associates called the Van Daans, with their teenage son Peter. They were later joined by a dentist named Dussel.

Anne noted everything that happened in a diary, and to make the entries more personal she wrote them in the form of letters to a made-up friend called Kitty.

On Wednesday, 8 July 1942, Anne naively wrote about the beginning of the crisis:

'Dear Kitty,

'Years seemed to have passed between Sunday and now. So much has happened, it is just as if the whole world had turned upside down. But I am still alive, Kitty, and that is the main thing, Daddy says.'

Anne goes on to tell 'Kitty' about the momentous events that took place on that sunny Sunday afternoon when their lives were changed for ever by the ringing of the doorbell.

'Margot appeared at the kitchen door looking very excited. "The SS have sent a call-up notice for Daddy," she whispered. "Mummy has gone to see Mr Van Daan immediately." (Van Daan is a friend who works with Daddy in the business.) It was a great shock to me, a call-up; everyone knows what that means.'

Their father was out and they were very concerned for him, but when the bell rang again Margot held Anne back. Thankfully it was not the SS.

During that long hot afternoon, each time the bell went, Margot and Anne crept softly down to see if it was their father. They were too afraid to answer the door to anyone else. Though he did later return home safely, for months afterwards the bell was to be the harbinger of doom, the chief source of concern to both families. But when the Van Daans called, they brought with them appalling news.

Margot and Anne were sent out of the room because Mr Van Daan wanted to talk to their mother alone. Later Mrs Frank spoke to Margot, and later still Margot told her sister. The call-up was not for their father, but for her. Anne was terrified and began to cry. Margot was sixteen; surely the Nazis wouldn't take anyone of that age. Anne could now see how vital it was for the Frank family to go into hiding. As to exactly where the hiding place would be, Mr Frank had refused to confide in his family so far, and no one was allowed to ask any questions.

Margot and Anne began to pack their most important belongings into school satchels. Anne immediately put in her diary. This was followed by hair-curlers, handkerchiefs, school books, a comb, old letters. Essentially, Anne took things that would make her remember their past lives. *'Memories mean more to me than dresses,'* she confided to her diary.

The next day, Thursday, 9 July, the family walked in the pouring rain to the office and the hiding place that had been prepared for them. Because of the call-up, the plan had had to be speeded up by ten days so the rooms were not as well organized as Mr Frank would have liked. Nevertheless, there was no chance of staying at home as the Gestapo could soon be taking action against them.

Mr Frank had four people working for him: Kraler, Koophuis, Miep, and Elli Vossen, a 23-year-old typist. They all knew about the hiding place but Mr Vossen, Elli's father, and two boys who worked in the warehouse didn't. It was important to limit the ring of trust to as few people as possible.

There was a large warehouse on the ground floor which was used as a store. The front door to the house was next to the warehouse door, and inside the front door was a second doorway, leading to a staircase. At the top of the stairs there was another door, with a frosted-glass window and the word 'Office' written in black letters. That was where Elli, Miep, and Mr Koophuis worked. Another small room contained a safe, a wardrobe and a large cupboard. A second office led off it which Kraler and Van Daan occupied. It was possible to reach this from the passage, but only via a glass door which could only be opened easily from the inside.

From there a long passage went past the coal store, up four steps into the showroom – and an inner sanctum which was full of dark furniture, with linoleum and carpets on the floor. Next door there was a large kitchen with a hot-water geyser and a gas stove. Then the toilet.

A wooden staircase led from the downstairs passage to the floor above where there was a small landing with a door at each end. The left one led to a store-room at the front of the house and to the attics.

The right-hand door finally led to the 'Secret Annexe' as they called it, and it would be hard for anyone to guess how many rooms lay hidden behind that plain grey door. This was exactly why Mr Frank chose his own offices as the hiding place for his family. The labyrinthine architecture concealed so much and could not be detected easily from outside or inside.

There was a steep staircase immediately opposite the entrance and on the left a small passage led into a room that was to become the Franks' bed-sitting-room. Next door was a smaller room, study and bedroom. On the right there was a toilet, with another door leading to Margot's and Anne's room. Up the next flight of stairs was another large and airy room with a gas stove and a sink. This area was to be the Van Daans' quarters, combining living-room, dining-room, and scullery. Finally, the small corridor room would become Peter Van Daan's apartment.

The greatest care had to be taken, both day and night, not to be seen or heard, and for a lively girl of thirteen this was to prove extremely difficult, and despite the size of the secret annexe the two families – and later the dentist – were going to spend a long time living together in the most intimate conditions which inevitably resulted in a considerable amount of stress. The dentist in particular caused a great deal of annoyance as his chief place of retreat was to be the lavatory seat.

On 9 August 1943, Anne noted in her diary: *'Three, four, five times a day someone stands impatiently in front of the door and wriggles, hopping from one foot to the other, hardly able to contain himself. Does it disturb him? Not a bit! From quarter-past seven till half-past, from half-past twelve till one o'clock, from two till quarter-past, from four till quarter-past, from six till quarter-past, and from half-past eleven until twelve. One can make a note of it – these are the regular "sitting times". He won't come off or pay any heed to an imploring voice at the door, giving warning of approaching disaster!'*

Anne passed the time by reading books, secretly

delivered by Dutch friends, and writing up her journal and was surprisingly adaptable, always retaining her optimism. She was religious, certain that God would protect her.

Soon another distraction alleviated her boredom. Anne slowly began to fall in love with Peter Van Daan. At first he was difficult and touchy, and she found it hard to take him seriously. He was a hypochondriac and always minutely observing his own health. After a year and a half, however, they began to talk and Anne realized that her fellow-prisoner was a very different person from the one she had so impatiently dismissed.

On 6 January 1944, Anne confided to her journal:

'Dear Kitty,

'My longing to talk to someone became so intense that somehow or other I took it in my head to choose Peter.

'Sometimes if I've been upstairs into Peter's room during the day, it always struck me as very snug, but because Peter is so retiring and would never turn anyone out who became a nuisance, I never dared stay long, because I was afraid he might think me a bore. I tried to think of an excuse to stay in his room and get him talking, without it being too noticeable, and my chance came yesterday.'

Peter loved doing crossword puzzles so Anne sat down and helped him. Gazing into his eyes as they sat there, opposite each other, she could sense his incipient manhood, his anxiety about how to behave and his intense shyness.

This particular evening passed without them being able to talk in any depth but later, when she was in bed, Anne decided to go and sit with him more often and try to get him to open up.

'Whatever you do, don't think I'm in love with Peter – not bit of it!' she pleads. *'If the Van Daans had had a daughter instead of a son, I should have tried to make friends with her too.'*

In fact, Anne *was* in love with Peter, a love that was to grow so intensely for both of them that the other prisoners in the secret annexe were soon to realize – with mixed feelings – what was going on between the two young people.

In March 1944, looking back over her period of captivity, Anne acutely observed the various changes that had happened to her:

'I look upon my life up till the New Year, as it were, through a powerful magnifying-glass. The sunny life at home, then coming here in 1942, the sudden change, the quarrels, the bickerings. I couldn't understand it, I was taken by surprise.'

At first she was a child, reacting to the insecurity and frustration of her circumstances with rudeness and outbreaks of crying, but after about six months she began to mature, coming to the conclusion that *'the others no longer had the right to throw me about like an india-rubber ball. I wanted to change in accordance with my own desires. But* one *thing that struck me even more was when I realized that even Daddy would never become my confidant over everything. I didn't want to trust anyone but myself any more.'*

She began to think and write stories and found that she was beginning to throw off her despondency.

By January 1944 she had discovered the joy of being in love. Still deeply religious she thanked God each night for *'all that is good and dear and beautiful'*, for her good health and above all for Peter.

'I don't think then of all the misery, but of the beauty that still remains,' she confided to her diary. *'This is one of the things that Mummy and I are so entirely different about. Her counsel when one feels melancholy is: "Think of all the misery in the world and be thankful that you are not sharing it!" My advice is: "Go outside, to the fields, enjoy nature and the sunshine, go out and try to recapture happiness in yourself and in God. Think of all the beauty that's still left in and around you and be happy!'*

Sadly, for Anne this was not to be. On 4 August 1944, German Security Police, together with Dutch Nazis, raided Otto Frank's office and forced one of his employees to show them the entrance to the secret annexe. Somehow their suspicions had been aroused – or there had been some kind of tip-off.

'To our great horror and regret we hear that the attitude of a great many people towards us Jews has changed. We hear that there is anti-semitism now in circles that never thought of it before. This news has affected us all very, very deeply. The cause of this hatred of the Jews is understandable, even human sometimes, but not good. The Christians blame the Jews for giving secrets away to the Germans, for betraying their helpers and for the fact that, through the Jews, a great many Christians have gone the way of so many others before them and suffered terrible punishments and a dreadful fate.'

All the 'prisoners' of the secret annexe were arrested and sent first to Westerbork, which was the main German concentration camp in Holland. They were then taken in cattle trucks to Auschwitz in German-occupied Poland.

Van Daan died there in the gas chambers, and at the end of the war Peter Van Daan, with a large number of other prisoners, was evacuated from the camp by the Germans. He was never heard of again.

In November 1944, two months before her

mother's death, Anne and Margot were sent to Bergen-Belsen in Germany. Anne remained optimistic in the face of appalling suffering, but in February 1945 both she and Margot caught typhus fever.

Margot lay in the bunk above Anne. Attempting to get up, she fell. The shock was too much for her and she died.

With her death, Anne's hope was finally extin-

guished and she too died a few days later.

Otto Frank, however, narrowly escaped death in the gas chambers of Auschwitz and was released by the Soviet Army on 27 January 1945.

After being arrested and tried more than once (and spending some years in jail) for subversive activities as a leader of the African National Congress, campaigning against the South African government, Nelson Mandela was sentenced to life imprisonment on Robben Island. Days were filled with hard manual labour and, like the other prisoners, he was utterly exhausted at the end of the day, the only personal advantage being that he slept deeply. Initially, letters and visits could only be made twice a year, but by 1981 two letters and two visits were allowed each month, although even then each written or spoken word was subjected to severe censorship. To aid the censor, the spoken and written words had to be very distinctly said or written. As a result, both prisoner and visitor soon learnt the art of the double meaning.

The prison on Robben Island, during the time of Nelson Mandela's incarceration, was highly punitive. The policy was to break the human spirit, to exploit human weakness, undermine human strength, destroy initiative and individuality, negate intelligence and produce a robot-like population of prisoners. In Mandela's view the great challenge was how to resist and *not* to adjust and become institutionalized. Above all he strove to keep intact the knowledge of the outside society and to live by its rules. He knew this was the only way to preserve one's personality. The survival of all the prisoners depended on this protective defiance, as much as their ability to share it with each other. Naturally, their responses to the various hardships differed. They were all living under incredible stress, but some were more capable of handling that stress than others.

Mandela remembers that the worst part of imprisonment was solitary confinement. Here, he came face to face with time and *'there is nothing more terrifying than to be alone with sheer time. Then the ghosts come crowding in. They can be very sinister, very mischievous, raising a thousand doubts in your mind about the people outside, their loyalty. Was your sacrifice worth the trouble? What would your life have been like if you hadn't got involved?'*

Mandela realized that it was only the individual who could save himself or herself. He also believed everyone has a latent talent for survival which will come to the fore under test. Often the prisoner is unaware of this talent because there is so much going on in life outside that it may remain buried, but in prison the talent can become a lifeline.

Some men on Robben Island were good with their hands and others good with their minds. A few excelled at both. Jeff Masemola was one such prisoner. He taught Mandela maths and he made a master key that would open any prison door. Eventually Masemola was removed from the general section because he was too ingenious and therefore too dangerous. Other prisoners, however, were equally ingenious, making their own tools with pieces of zinc and whatever they found. They brought back what appeared to be debris from the workplace, bits of wood and stone, and during lock-up time fashioned these into exquisite pieces of sculpture or furniture. The human spirit, the will to survive, was clearly demonstrated by their actions.

Mandela, with his great gifts for seeking out the positive and the spiritual in his fellow prisoners, also noticed that amongst them were some men who were prepared to make every possible sacrifice for their fellows, and they came from a wide variety of political groups. In the course of time, the prisoners established committees which were disciplinary, educational, political, recreational and literary. The most important point in humanitarian terms, however, was that the authorities came to recognize, unofficially, that in the final analysis, order in the prison was preserved, not by the warders, but by the prisoners themselves.

They had to build their own social life and modelled it on the way they had lived and would live again outside the prison walls. Above all, they encouraged study, sharing disciplines and expertise. In fact they placed highest value on sharing every resource they had. Mandela feels that on the whole they succeeded.

To view Nelson Mandela's suffering more objectively, the conditions on Robben Island are described here by Strini Moodley, one of the nine members of the South African Student Organization who were convicted in 1976 for terrorism by 'thought'. None of the nine had committed any act of terrorism whatsoever, but the court found their speeches, drama and poetry worthy of sentences to Robben Island.

They arrived on Robben Island on 22 December 1976, looking forward to meeting leaders like Mandela who were their legendary heroes, the only plus factor of their long-term sentences. They were not to meet them for some time, however, as the policy was to keep them apart.

The section Strini Moodley and his companions had been placed in had not been used for a while and was referred to as the observation or punishment section. The place was so damp that the paintwork was peeling off. If anyone kept their foot on the cement floor for ten or fifteen minutes and then lifted it up, a puddle of water was usually revealed.

A passage ran down the centre of the block, with the cells on either side, and the warden's office was at one end of the passage. Beyond was a small walled-in yard with six showers and a couple of toilet pans. There was no hot water.

Their cells were small, about three paces each way, and the only light came from high windows. From one of them, a glass pane had been removed so that the wardens could check what they were doing. The windows were barred from the inside and all Moodley could see from his back window was the concrete walls of other cell blocks.

Facilities included a sanitary bucket, a face cloth, a bottle, a towel, three sleeping mats (one grass and two felt) and four blankets. The squalid space and its belongings was Moodley and his friends' world for the next six weeks. They were let out for an hour each day: in the morning to shower and use the toilets, and in the afternoon to breathe fresh air and stretch their limbs.

Once in the yard, they immediately defied the warders, loudly shouting 'Amandla!' so they could make contact with the other prisoners. Because they wouldn't stop, the authorities built a high wall.

On the day before Christmas they were visited by Ahmed Kathrada and Frank Anthony of the Non-European Unity Movement. They brought tobacco and sweets. Kathrada asked to see Moodley, telling him that he knew his father.

They discussed how they could establish communication with the other prisoners and in particular Mandela. They had already discovered a gap in the iron gate between their yards and thought it would be possible to leave messages there. '*We told Kathy we wanted to see Nelson and suggested that he should stand in their yard at a certain spot at a certain time when we were outside in our yard, so we could identify him. At the time of his arrest, most of us had been toddlers and some not yet born, but he was part of our psyche and our political culture and we were most anxious to see him.*'

Mandela complied with their request, and they saw him standing, tall, slim and regal. They didn't speak or make any signs, but simply looked with considerable wonder at the man who was the leader of suppressed black society in South Africa – the man on whom they had pinned all their hopes of freedom.

Moodley and his group were later moved to Section 'D', a communal block that was a little more civilized. The toilets and showers were inside so they had continuous access to them rather than having to wait for the appointed hour, and much more importantly they had each other's company. At night they talked, planned activities, read or studied whatever material was not restricted.

The most unpleasant forms of hard labour on

Robben Island were collecting bird droppings and lime quarrying. The bird droppings made them dirty and smell so pungent that they could hardly bear their own bodies at the end of the day.

At the quarries, the sun shone on the white lime and blinded their eyes. As a result, Moodley could hardly see. They were expected to extract the lime, shovel and load it without a break. The prisoners requested rests but the warders refused. The argument intensified and they went on strike.

A reinforcement of warders arrived and the 150 prisoners were ordered to return to work. They still refused and were returned to their cells. That evening, just as they began to eat supper, they were ordered to stop. The prisoners

protested and the dogs were immediately set on them. Bitten, bloodied, but furiously angry they picked up picks and spades and lashed out. A further reinforcement of warders followed who baton-charged and overpowered the now seventy-plus rioting prisoners. As a result they were locked up in Section 'C'.

Nelson Mandela sent them notes of encouragement and support, and when the rioters went on a hunger strike Mandela and his group joined them. Eventually the Red Cross intervened and the hunger strike was called off.

But the situation was not to end there. A magistrate was brought in from the mainland and eight of the prisoners went on trial, including Moodley, but in the end the charge against them was withdrawn. At all times they received support and advice from Mandela.

Later, Moodley, now moved permanently into 'B' Section, got to know Nelson Mandela personally. *'He came up to all my expectations. He stood head and shoulders above the others. Everyone looked up to him and respected him. When he spoke, we listened. He was patient, tolerant and I never saw him lose his temper.'*

He was keen to understand Moodley and his group's political approach, and arranged for them to present papers so they could understand the Black Consciousness movement at first hand.

Moodley felt that Mandela had few problems identifying with their position, but was, at the same time, constructively critical. When he expressed the opinion that Moodley and his group were somewhat rash, *'I suggested that what he really meant was that we were just a little more radical. I told him my father used to say I was rash, but finally conceded that I was more radical than he was. Nelson did not argue against that.'*

Mandela's tolerance of the different attitudes that prevailed amongst the political prisoners at Robben Island was remarkable, and Moodley found him much more liberal than his contemporaries. Moodley remembered a film that was shown to the prisoners to impress upon them differences between good and evil – and the rightness of the South African State. It showed two groups of men: a group of bikers and an army contingent. The army went to so-called heroic war in Vietnam. They were acting within the official law; the bikers broke the law at every opportunity, ending in rape and molestation. The army caught up with them, and the film concluded with the bikers being arrested by the army.

There was unanimous agreement at the end of the film that the bikers deserved their punishment, but Moodley disagreed, pointing out the propagandist symbolism of the film. He alleged the bikers represented the revolutionary youth of the 1970s. He went on to say that the film condoned institutionalized violence, but condemned anti-system violence. Immediately the other prisoners verbally attacked him, accusing him of supporting a group of evil rapists, but Nelson Mandela disagreed and said that Moodley might well have a point. He suggested he should be asked to prepare a paper on the subject. Moodley did as he suggested and there was considerable debate, in which Mandela played a key part.

Nelson Mandela has been one of the most discussed political leaders of this century and his life and writings are very familiar. But Moodley's account of his time on Robben Island gives us a glimpse of a true leader's survival instincts as well as his personal dedication to democracy. Mandela was a man of exceptional stature who had been imprisoned for well over twenty years, remaining civilized and open-minded throughout his ordeal. Nelson Mandela also managed to re-enter the outside world with all its personal and public pressures and to become a powerful, dedicated leader. To govern is always a far cry from spear-heading an opposition, but drawing on the survival techniques and knowledge of priorities developed during his long years of confinement Mandela has proved himself as one of the most important leaders of our time.

BIBLIOGRAPHY

BAILEY, Maurice and Maralyn, *117 Days Adrift*. Nautical Publishing Co., 1974.

BLASHFORD-SNELL, John, *Where the Trail Runs Out*. Hutchinson, 1974.

BLES, Mark and LOW, Robert, *The Kidnap Business*. Pelham Books, 1987.

BONINGTON, Chris, *The Everest Years*. Hodder & Stoughton, 1986.

CHAPMAN, Abraham, *Steal Away*. Ernest Benn, 1971.

COLLINS, Michael, *Flying to the Moon*. Robson, 1979.

CRAME, Chris and HARRIS, Sim. *Hostage*. Clare Books, 1982.

DI GIOVANNI, Janine, *The Quick and the Dead: Under Siege in Sarajevo*. Phoenix House, 1994

FIENNES, Ranulf, *Mind over Matter. The Epic Crossing of the Antarctic Continent*. Sinclair-Stevenson, 1993.

FRANK, Anne, *The Diary of Anne Frank*. Pan Books, 1954.

GERAGHTY, Tony, *Who Dares Wins. The Story of the Special Air Service, 1950-1980*. Arms & Armour Press, 1980.

HEWITT, Gavin, *Terry Waite. Why was he kidnapped?* Bloomsbury, 1991.

MACK, Joanna and HUMPHRIES, Steve, *London at War*. Sidgwick & Jackson, 1985.

MARIOTT, John, *Disaster at Sea*. Ian Allen, 1987.

MATTHIESSEN, Peter, *The Cloud Forest. A Chronicle of the South American Wilderness*. Collins Harvill, 1961.

McCARTHY, John and MORRELL, Jill, *Some Other Rainbow*. Bantam Press, 1993.

McCRUM, Robert, 'My Old and New Lives', in *The New Yorker*, May 27, 1996.

MEER, Fatima, *Higher Than Hope. The Authorised Biography of Nelson Mandela*. Hamish Hamilton, 1988.

NEILL, Robert, *SOS – The Story Behind the Army Expedition to Borneo's Death Valley*. Century, 1995.

BIBLIOGRAPHY

PETERS, John and NICHOL, John, *Tornado Down*. Michael
  Joseph, 1992.

READ, Piers Paul, *Alive. The Story of the Andes Survivors*.
  Secker & Warburg, 1974.

RIDGEWAY, John, *Flood Tide*. Hodder & Stoughton, 1988.

SHACKLETON, *His Antarctic writings selected and introduced
  by Christopher Ralling*. BBC, 1983.

THE MAIL ON SUNDAY, 'Hostages in the Stone Age': interviews
  with Daniel Start, Anna McIvor, Annette van der Kolk and Bill
  Oates. May 26th, 1996.

TOOTELL, Betty, *'All Four Engines Have Failed'*. André
  Deutsch, 1985.

WESTALL, Robert, *Children of the Blitz*. Viking, 1985.

WESTON, Simon, *Walking Tall*. Bloomsbury, 1989.

WIGHTON, Suzy, *One Day at a Time*. Hutchinson, 1990.